THE STORY OF
COMPUTING

THE STORY OF
COMPUTING

From the Abacus to Artificial Intelligence

Dermot Turing

ARCTURUS

ARCTURUS

This edition published in 2018 by Arcturus Publishing Limited
26/27 Bickels Yard, 151–153 Bermondsey Street,
London SE1 3HA

ISBN: 978-1-78828-030-3
AD005781UK

Printed in China

CONTENTS

SOLVING PROBLEMS

'Computing is not about computers anymore. It is about living.'

Nicholas Negroponte, 1995

Computers are everywhere, secretly shaping our lives. It is difficult to remember how we lived without them. The way in which computers have become integrated into every aspect of society, and the speed with which the transition has occurred, is truly remarkable. This breadth and depth of change has brought about a transformation, not just of society, but of how we perceive computers themselves. What computers are actually for has changed, along with the way we use them. So what, in fact, is computing?

Men and women have been dealing with mathematical problems since civilization first emerged. It was not long before they sought to create machines to help them.

Counting conundrums

A deceptively simple answer to the question is provided by the 1944 edition of the *Shorter Oxford Dictionary*:

> Compute, v. 1631. 1. trans. To determine by calculation; to reckon, count; to take account of.

Historically, computing was about problem-solving, especially where the problems involved complex scientific calculations. Computing is often regarded as an aspect of mathematics, as early computing was mostly about arithmetic. Sometimes arithmetic boils down to counting, but counting is only one aspect of computing. Here's the problem. It's all fine to know that my field contains 12 grazing animals, but I need more information, specifically whether there are any rams in the field as well as ewes, how many lambs there are and when they were born and so on, and that information does not readily come from counting.

What computing involves, as well as counting, is sorting. Modern computing is about recognition and choice-making as much as mathematical operations. Problems requiring demanding computational solutions continued to grow and become more involved: navigation, decryption,

Agriculture required a certain amount of arithmetic. Knowing how many animals of each sex was important for early farmers. But there is more to computing than counting.

forecasting of all sorts, all inviting a faster approach to computing and this led to mechanization.

When societies grew large enough to require a sophisticated government, one of the first priorities was the need to quantify and to measure. For example, they needed to know the number of people there were in order to tax them, or the amount of farm produce available for trade and commerce, or to track the passage of the sun, moon and stars, so as to better understand the gods. So it quickly became necessary to have assistance from people skilled in the ability to carry out the necessary calculations. Computing was then about helping with the complicated but needful aspects of government, commerce and religion.

Men and machines

The people who carried out this hard work were called 'computers' – because they made the calculations or 'computations'.

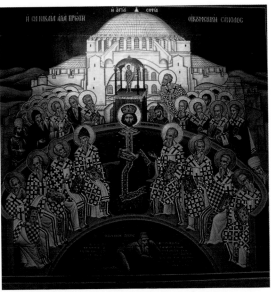

With Christianity came the need to calculate the date for Easter. The First Council of Nicaea in AD325 established that a common date should be observed and a method for computing it was established.

When the 18th-century Astronomer Royal Nevil Maskelyne compiled the first nautical almanac, used until recent times for navigation at sea, he co-ordinated the output of a network of computers working from homes all over the UK who produced the necessary calculations (see page 28). Similarly, the 19th-century US astronomer Edward Charles Pickering of the Harvard College Observatory recruited a team of exclusively female computers to compile the Henry Draper Star Catalog to list some 10,000 stars.

But even that does not quite capture it. I do not use my computer as a super-fast sorter or a calculator very often. Much of the time I use it to get information and for e-mail. Computers still have their role in big calculations, and in controlling machinery and complex systems such as the electricity

Edward Charles Pickering, working for the Harvard College Observatory, recruited a team of women as computers to help assemble the Henry Draper Star Catalog.

grid, but for most people they are a means of accessing the Internet and keeping in touch with friends. Today, computing can mean information and communications technology (ICT), which once described encyclopaedias and the telephone, neither of which had anything to do with computing. The truth is that computing is so versatile that it has been able to move into these areas. Computing is also behind new expansions into data science, artificial intelligence, and cybernetics. These are a far cry from difficult exercises in arithmetic.

The changing world

Once computing had escaped from a cage that equated it with calculating, a redefinition was needed. Just as 'cyber' ceased to be a label associated with robotics, 'computing' redefined itself as information and communications technology. But computing is different from telecommunications and it is different from data transfer, although it sits alongside these things and empowers them. Maybe computing has become subsumed, for many people, into data science. But there are still universities where people study 'pure' computation – the topic invented by Alan Turing in his paper from 1936, which also set out a blueprint for a programmable computing machine.

This book traces the development of computing from its origins in

Once computers became programmable, effective coding could be used to apply their processing power to almost any problem.

electronics speeded up and miniaturized computing, making it possible to do far more with computing machinery than had been imagined early civilization to the present day, and before. In the 21st century, the explosion perhaps beyond. The story of computing happened: suddenly, computing was about starts with astrolabes and abacuses, and everything.

why people needed those things. Later, The story of computing is not about machinery became more complicated and dull steel boxes sitting in the store-room of directed towards improvements in the a museum. It's as much about ideas and the basic problems of arithmetic and sorting. society in which we live, and the route we In the 20th century, the emergence of took to get here.

Computers have grown ever faster and more impressive – but there is more to computing than steel boxes.

Chapter 1

A IS FOR ABACUS

Computing machinery dates back to the earliest times in history. Devices helped people solve complicated problems, with a strong focus on astronomy. Later, as arithmetic became more involved and abstracted, the algorithms for computing changed direction, and the devices became associated more with numerical calculations. Calculations became more complex, and computing became a specialized occupation.

Astronomy provided the earliest catalyst for creating computing machines. Here, Ottoman scholars use a variety of instruments in the Istanbul Observatory.

A is for abacus. Or maybe for astrolabe, or for the Antikythera mechanism, or for any number of antiquated devices used for computing. Humans have been designing problem-solving machines since the earliest days of civilization. In a sense, all machines are built to solve problems, such as raising water from deep underground or lifting heavy loads. Eventually, the specifically intellectual problems of arithmetic, measurement and astronomical prediction also proved amenable to mechanical help.

So what distinguishes these devices from other remarkable ancient artefacts? What

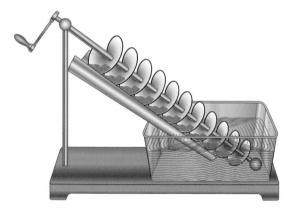

The Archimedes Screw was an ingenious creation, but unlike computing machines, it was not able to provide answers to problems.

about dividers, plumblines, set-squares and so forth? These are all clever machines that assist people with practical problems in navigation, surveying and engineering by helping with the creation and checking of data. But they lack one central feature: none of these devices is able to give its user the answer to a problem. That is because these objects are not involved in the process of computing.

Astronomical answers

The Assyrians may not have been the first to develop serious computing techniques, but thanks to their habit of preserving their works on clay tablets, much of their thinking – in particular, their thinking about mathematics – has survived. Their ability to manipulate highly complex numerical problems – including fractions, square roots, quadratic equations, and more – implies a great deal of sophistication in their society. Their work extended to the measurement and division of the day and of the circle, concepts that have been in continuous use ever since.

Religion has often been closely connected with astronomy. It was self-evident that the sun moved around the earth once a day (or appeared to, anyway), but the behaviour of other heavenly bodies was more complicated. Although the moon waxes and wanes every four weeks and affects the tides and the level of coastal waters in predictable

This Star Chart from Sumeria, dated c.3300BC, was used for astrological calculations.

The Hanging Gardens of Babylon were one of the wonders of the ancient world and required extraordinarily advanced engineering that reflected the mathematical proficiency of the Babylonians.

ASSYRIAN ANGLE

The Hanging Gardens of Babylon were justly ranked among the seven wonders of the ancient world. The engineering required to create the terraces and to irrigate them was more advanced than other societies could achieve. For in Mesopotamia, the successive cultures (Assyrian, Persian, Sumerian and many others) honoured one particular attribute: their mathematical system.

Unlike modern systems, the Babylonian approach to mathematics was based on the number 60, probably because 60 is divisible by so many convenient 'factors' (the whole numbers that can be multiplied to make bigger numbers), namely 2, 3, 4, 5, 6, 10, 12, 15, 20 and 30. The Babylonian numerical system relied on one-sixtieth as its basic fraction and $1/3600$ (that is, $1/60$ squared) then $1/216000$ ($1/60$ cubed) for greater detail. They were able to calculate $\sqrt{2}$ as $1 + 24/60 + 50/3600 + 10/216000$, which comes out in decimal notation as 1.414222, within a cat's whisker of the modern value of 1.414214. They also invented 'positional numeration' – a way of writing numbers so that their relative location indicates their value, so that 12 means twelve and 21 means twenty-one, even though the individual symbols are the same and simply mean 1 and 2. They also had a representation of zero, which is an important 'place holder' in maths and without which, more complex calculations would not be possible.

Many of their intellectual achievements perished amid the successive wars fought for mastery of their valuable territory. But one thing endured, even if the concept of zero had to be re-created later. That was the division of units of time and angle into sixtieths – hours having 60 minutes and minutes 60 seconds, and degrees having the same subdivisions. The decimalizers of the General Conference on Weights and Measures, which co-ordinates and standardizes the SI units of measurement, would no doubt be much happier with a decimal system for arcs and time, but the Babylonian system is just too firmly embedded.

A tablet filled with cuneiform numerals. The Babylonians based their numerical system on the number 60, the influence of which can still be seen today in the length of hours and minutes.

ways, working out where and when it will appear in the sky is more difficult. And then there are eclipses. These have often been seen as troublesome events, the harbingers of disaster, and need to be predicted in order to prepare appropriate propitiations. The minor stars and planets are even more complex. To keep on top of this required years of study. Prediction, in a pre-algebra era, needed machinery.

Devices to assist with astronomical computing were developed in many continents and in many cultures. The Mayans compiled data and calculations related to astronomy as long ago as the 9th century BC, using a catalogue of such information to make predictions about

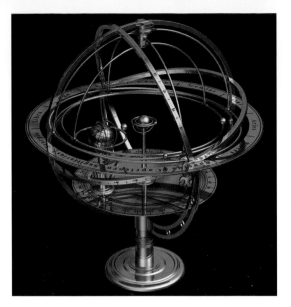

Armillary spheres were used to model the movements of the heavens and placed earth at the centre of the universe. They were found across the world, in ancient Greece, China and the Islamic world.

eclipses, the phases of the moon and the movements of the planets. The ancient Greeks and Chinese each invented forms of 'armillary sphere' to demonstrate the motion of stars about the earth.

At the end of the 10th century AD, the Persian astronomer Abu Mahmud Hamid ibn al-Khidr Al-Khujandi constructed a huge sextant-like device near Tehran to measure the earth's tilt. In Samarkand, in the early 15th century, Jamshid al-Kashi developed machinery to predict the alignment of planets. The list could go on, but perhaps the most famous is the

The ancient Mayan observatory at El Caracol was one of many buildings used to help predict eclipses, the phases of the moon and the movement of the planets.

complex Antikythera mechanism, which has been called the world's oldest computer.

At the Museum of the History of Science in Oxford there is an astonishing collection of 'astrolabes' (see box, p.16). Astrolabes are used to determine the angle of elevation of stars. The elevation of a particular astronomical body varies with latitude and so the device could help travellers identify their location. The earliest astrolabe in the Oxford collection dates from around AD900 and was made in Syria or Egypt. As Islamic culture percolated into Europe via southern Spain, along with it came Islamic knowledge, equipment and computation. One of the earliest astrolabes in the Oxford collection dates from around AD1300, with star pointers in the form of birds with long beaks. Astrolabes of increasing decorative quality and sophistication

ANTIKYTHERA MECHANISM

In 1901, divers put on Victorian underwater gear and descended 20m (66ft) below the surface of the sea off the Greek island of Antikythera. There lay a wrecked Greek ship, dating from before the Christian era, packed full of treasures such as statues of bronze and marble, furniture, amphorae and more. Tucked away amid all this was an obscure device, approximately 14cm (5.5in) in diameter, made partly of wood and partly of metal, now corroded. But what metal! The box-like object was a machine, made of interacting gear-wheels, precisely tooled so as to turn in line with the heavens.

Discovering the function of the machine required new techniques: as the 20th century ran on, new techniques became available and new professors came up with new theories as to what it did and how. A consensus, based on images produced by CT (computerized tomography) scans, conventional X-rays, photography and good old-fashioned counting of gear teeth, has emerged.

The machine was operated by a handle on its side. Turning the handle rotated the gears to show, on display dials on its front face, the positions of the sun, the moon and the planets, the date and the phase of the moon. At the back, the month and year and timing of eclipses were displayed on an imaginative spiral dial.

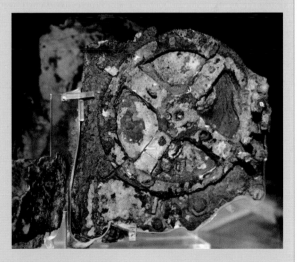

The Antikythera Mechanism is perhaps the world's oldest computer. Dating from c.100BC, the clockwork mechanism was used to predict the movement of the sun, the stars, the moon and the planets.

began to be created in Europe around the time of the Renaissance, though their accuracy for navigation at sea was poor when compared with other instruments such as a sextant. For people of Islamic faith, the direction of Mecca is a necessary calculation; an astrolabe can be used for that purpose. Astrolabes are probably better classified as aids to measurement rather than computational devices, but the contrary argument can be made since (like the Antikythera mechanism) they provide short-cuts for the user, with much information and the product of accumulated knowledge stored within their dials and scales.

Another astronomical device that falls between measurement and computation is the clock. We may not ordinarily think of a clock as a means to observe the behaviour of the heavens but, as the Assyrians taught us, the division of a day into equal parts is a natural progression from an observation of the sun's movement. Telling the time using an instrument such as a sundial or a water-clock is unlikely to

ASTROLABE

An astrolabe typically consists of a shallow dish (the 'mater') containing several flat discs, each of which is engraved with a squashed-out projection of the heavens as seen from a particular position on the earth. The outside edge is marked with a scale of degrees or time-units so that the device can be correctly aligned. One disc corresponds with the user's latitude. Over this sits an elaborately shaped wheel, pierced like a frame, which can be rotated according to the time of day. On this wheel is a smaller circle; as the wheel rotates, the part of the sky visible at a given time is revealed. The pierced wheel is called the 'rete' and it usually has pointers to indicate the positions of major stars. On top of the mater, the discs and the rete, some astrolabes have something that looks like the long hand of a clock, called the 'rule', which may have sights to assist with observations.

Astrolabes were navigational devices used to determine the angle of elevation of the stars. From their origins in the 10th century AD, they soon became an essential tool for sailors across the world.

A string is threaded through the top of the device so that the instrument hangs vertically. You can find the time of day (or night) by lining up the rule with the sun (or a star) and checking its altitude against a scale on the back of the device. Or you can find the time of sunrise, the length of a day or, by using a special disc, it is possible to convert an observation about the elevation of a star into information about the user's latitude.

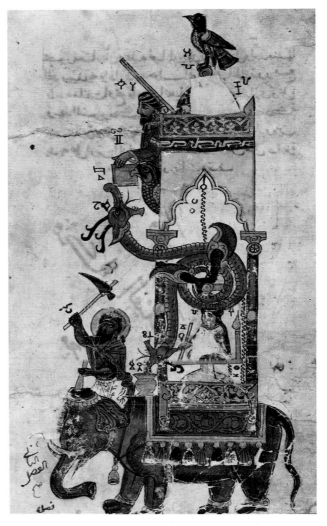

Clocks came in all shapes and sizes. The striking 'Elephant Clock' was designed by Al-Jazari in the 12th century AD and was one of many ingenious approaches to the problem of calculating time.

be regarded as an exercise in computing. But when you consider the complexity of a modern mechanical clock with an escapement, spring- or weight-driven motion and gearing to convert motion to a read-out on the clock's face, the distinction becomes fuzzy. The machine is actually computing the time, rather than relying on the passage of time to give you an observation: were it not so, clocks would not run fast or slow. The earliest mechanical clocks that compute, rather than measure, time, were invented in China in the 8th century AD. In Europe, clocks with escapements were put into many ecclesiastical buildings at the end of the 13th century AD, particularly in England, France and Italy.

It was not always the case that hours were of equal duration. Clock technology had to reflect this. Traditional Japanese time-keeping required the hours of daylight to be divided into six parts and the hours of darkness also to be so divided. As summer recedes into winter the durations of these parts will

change. Western engineering during the Japanese Edo period (1603–1868AD) had allowed clocks of immense beauty and accuracy to be developed for timekeeping of equal-length hours; the challenge to the engineers' ingenuity was to find a mechanism to handle the inequality of Japanese hours.

Pillar clocks do not have a Western-style circular face but a descending weight that

Clocks compute, rather than simply measure time. Innovation began in the churches, as can be seen in this clock from Salisbury Cathedral, which features an escapement.

passes markers as the day wears on. The markers can be adjusted according to the season or whether it is day or night. When the clock is wound, the weight is brought back to the start of its path.

Other types of Japanese clock do have a circular face. A curious example in the Seiko Museum in Tokyo has a rotating face, but fixed hands. Every day, at dawn and again at dusk, the weights that drive the mechanism that rotates the face must be adjusted slightly to ensure the time-keeping keeps pace with the changing seasons. Once Japanese culture was exposed to Western ideas – approximately at the same time as the Renaissance in Europe – this brought with it the notion of fixed-duration hours and mechanical European-style clocks. Soon after Japan ended its policy of isolation in 1873, the traditional Japanese method of time-keeping disappeared.

It all adds up

Equipment for predicting the behaviour of sun, moon and stars certainly had its place, but it was no help to ordinary folk trying to carry out the daily activities of commerce. The problems facing more ordinary people might have been esoteric and more mundane but they were vital. I can offer you horsebeans at four pence a sackful and I can also offer you dried peas at three pence a sackful. Alas, you know there is a greater chance of a bad pea contaminating part of the sack, but good peas can be sold to the Navy and generate a better profit. On the other hand, if I sell you the horsebeans, you know you can get a tolerable price for them if you travel to a distant village, but a night's stay there will cost money that needs to be taken off the profit. Which is the better deal, if you have only 12 pence to spend?

These are simple questions in arithmetic that in the modern day we have no difficulty in working through. But modern arithmetic is based on centuries of development of efficient systems of notation, both for algebra

ROMAN THIRD R

Without cheating (that is, without converting back to modern decimal notation and using modern methods), how would you add CXLVII and LXXXIX?

Based on counting-boards, it seems that the approach would have been something like this. The particular difficulty presented by Roman numerals is the abbreviated representation for numbers like 40 and 9 where there is an inherent subtraction (40 is XL, that is L minus X; 9 is IX, that is X minus I). The first step is to create a board that has three columns, one of which deals with the unit to be subtracted. This can be done for each of our two numbers, using blobs to represent stones or other tokens that would have been placed on a Roman counting board:

CXLVII		
unit	subtracted element	main number
C		•
I		•
X	•	
V		•
I		• •

+

LXXXIX		
unit	subtracted element	main number
C		
L		•
X		• • • •
V		
I	•	

Then the blobs for the two numbers can be amalgamated, and finally the blobs can be rearranged to arrive at the answer. Because two **L** is better written as **C**, a 'carry' is needed at the final stage.

unit	subtracted element	main number
C		•
L		• •
X	•	• • • •
V		•
I	•	• •

=

unit	subtracted element	main number
C		• •
L		
X		• • •
V		•
I		•

This approach to arithmetic, particularly where unequal-sized units were involved (such as gallons, pints and fluid ounces, or pounds, shillings and pence) was very persistent. Records indicate that governments and businesses were dependent on counting-board methods until mediaeval times (and the abandonment of Roman notation for numbers).

and for the actual numbers that algebraic methods can process. In ancient times these were lacking. Pity the poor Roman schoolchildren wrestling with arithmetic and using Roman numerals – geometry may have seemed easier.

The earliest devices for helping with arithmetic can be viewed as counting aids:

helping merchants keep tally and to add, subtract, multiply and divide. No surprise then that one of the most enduring and most wide-spread arithmetical aids is the 'abacus': a simple counting device that can perform all these operations. First invented in Babylon between 2700-2300BC and independently invented in China at least 1200 years before the start of the Christian era, the abacus is still in use today. Because it just keeps tally – in other words, its purpose is to help humans not lose count – it does not depend on any fancy notation or 'algorithms' (see page 21–2). Some modern explanations of how to 'use' an abacus merely translate modern algorithms for multiplication or addition to the beads on the abacus's wire. Such explanations may not be illegitimate, but they are probably anachronistic, just as multiplying XIV by IV can be done by converting the numbers back to Arabic style and using a modern method for achieving the result (14 × 4 = 56, so answer LVI) gets the answer, but not in the way the Romans did it.

More complex devices for assisting with arithmetical calculations needed to await the development of more sophisticated notation. It seems that Indian civilizations developed decimal notation towards the end of the 6th century AD and the concept reached Europe via the Islamic route a few centuries later. The idea of writing in decimals, with position (rather than a different symbol) representing an increase in power and with a special figure (zero) to denote a null space, thus became indelibly associated with the great Islamic mathematician and astronomer Muhammad ibn Musa al-Khwarizmi. (Muhammad ibn Musa was also the author of a book whose title *Hisob al-jabr wa'l muqabalah – The Compendious Book on Calculation by Completion and Balancing –* gave the word 'algebra' to the world.)

Believed to have been invented in Babylon nearly 4,500 years ago, the abacus was perhaps the earliest computing machine.

Muhammad ibn Musa was the inventor of the number '0' and algebra, which were essential to completing more complex calculations.

schoolchildren to learning their 'times-tables' by rote, progressing to long multiplication and eventually to that most fiendish of arithmetical horrors, long division. Let it be said at once that these things would not be necessary at all if humans were born with only one finger, since those operations are impossible in a binary system. But a binary system loses all the interest and attractions of the decimal system: some children enjoy finding the patterns that emerge from decimal numbers. The inversions, for instance, in the nine-times table

$1 \times 9 = 09$	$10 \times 9 = 90$
$2 \times 9 = 18$	$9 \times 9 = 81$
$3 \times 9 = 27$	$8 \times 9 = 72$
$4 \times 9 = 36$	$7 \times 9 = 63$
$5 \times 9 = 45$	$6 \times 9 = 54$

Once the new, simpler system for notation had come about, simpler techniques for arithmetical operations became possible, allowing numbers to be used in more and more ways, permeating all aspects of civilized life. With greater usage, the need for tools to speed up and improve the accuracy of number-crunching became all the greater and inventions began to spring up to help with calculation.

Digital school

The development of a decimal numbering system has condemned generations of

or the more complex and curious patterns observed in squares of numbers:

$$11^2 = 121;$$
$$12^2 = 144 \text{ and } 21^2 = 441;$$
$$13^2 = 169 \text{ and } 31^2 = 961.$$

For other people there is no such thing as having fun with numbers. Learning the technique for long multiplication is arduous. The traditional method is to multiply – using

Schickard's calculating machine was used for addition, subtraction, multiplication and division. In some ways, its capabilities superseded many of the adding machines that followed in later centuries.

those laboriously memorized times-tables – the first number, units first, by the units, then the tens, then the hundreds, and so on, then the second number, remembering the carries, and then do the same thing for the tens of the first number and so forth. This method is an algorithm – that is, the steps or rules to be followed in order to make a calculation or solve a problem.

Other algorithms are possible. For instance, as multiplication is nothing more than repeated addition until the number of repeats is equal to the multiplier, you could just keep on adding and press a counter each time you complete a sum. And the standard classroom algorithm for long division is, quite frankly, a total cheat: you do serial subtraction, but first of all you guess at a number to subtract, which is hardly an algorithm at all.

What this trip back to the schoolroom is telling us is that decimal arithmetic demanded the invention of algorithms to help with computation. Once simple algorithms were available, the nature of the problem changed to one of accuracy. Inventions that improved the accuracy of complex calculations were needed.

Enter John Napier, who might be called 'clever sticks' for his two important contributions to the simplification of arithmetical computation. First, he invented a set of sticks or rods – called 'Napier's Bones' – that can be used to perform multiplication. Those rods rely on the multiplication tables and convert into simpler steps the schoolroom algorithm for multiplication. Greater simplicity tends to greater accuracy. It is disappointing, then, to learn that Napier did not actually invent – or, certainly, was

John Napier, eighth Laird of Merchiston, a landowner, astronomer and mathematician, made a great contribution to computation in his discovery of logarithms.

was a Scottish aristocrat, born in 1550. His father was only 17 at the time, but when Mary, Queen of Scots was on the throne, there were far more peculiar goings-on in the kingdom. John Napier died in 1617 and there is some doubt about his burial-place, which might be the family vault in St Giles' Cathedral, or more likely St Cuthbert's church, in Edinburgh. But Napier's bones have nothing to do with his skeleton.

not the first to invent – the quick way of doing multiplication that is possible with his 'bones'. That seems to have happened in India in the 12th century AD and percolated through to Europe in succeeding centuries. But Napier's other invention, the logarithm, was a huge leap forward, if not a step-change in simplicity.

John Napier, eighth Laird of Merchiston,

'Napier's Bones' was a machine consisting of a series of rods that can be used for calculations using multiplication.

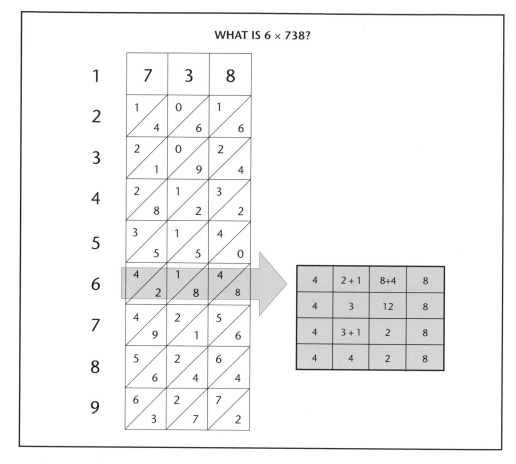

WHAT IS 6 × 738?

Napier's bones are a set of rods containing the multiplication tables from 0 to 9, squared off for each multiplier, with the units in the lower right separated from the tens in the upper left. When placed adjacent to each other, the numbers in the triangles drawn on the rods, or bones, can be read off in pairs along the diagonal and then added; any carries can go across and then the answer is arrived at. (You can do long-multiplication too using his bones, though this is not illustrated in the diagram above.)

Napier saw that adding the powers of numbers had the same effect as multiplication: $2^2 \times 2^3$ is 4 × 8, or 32, which can also be written as 2^{2+3}. Multiplication can be turned into addition if numbers can be represented as powers of the same base. In 1615, Henry Briggs, the Savilian Professor of Geometry at Oxford, visited John Napier in Scotland and they agreed that the logarithm method using base 10 (log 10 = 1) should be adopted as a standard; and it then fell to Briggs to begin the tedious and complex job of computing the logarithms of actual numbers. This was done by finding square roots using an algorithm known since Babylonian times.

The invention of logarithms led directly to the invention of the slide-rule as a device to speed up computation. Slide-rules enable addition of two numbers by sliding one scale along another and subtraction can follow a similar process. When the scale is logarithmic, the 'addition' is of powers or 'exponents'. The exponent is the number of times the 'variable' (the unknown number you are trying to find) is multiplied by itself – expressed, for example, like this: x^2

($x \times x$) or x^3 ($x \times x \times x$).) In a logarithmic scale the result to be read off is the product rather than the sum of the starting values. Slide-rules endured for centuries, until the development of affordable electronic calculators in the 1970s. So did another device for assisting with arithmetic: the adding machine.

Pascaline

Blaise Pascal's father was a tax-collector under the Ancien Régime of France. As an

---

SLIDE-RULE

A typical slide-rule shows a scale of numbers. On close examination, it is apparent that the numbers bunch together as they get larger: Napier envisaged exactly this pattern, imagining a moving point that covered less and less distance the further it was from the starting-point. On the slide, a similar scale of numbers is presented. To multiply, the slide is moved so that the 1 on the slide is next to the first number you want to multiply – say 21.5. Then, if the multiplier is, say, 4.45, that number is found on the scale of the slide and the product will be the number showing opposite on the fixed scale. Modern slide-rules were equipped with cursors to facilitate the accurate reading of results – in this case ninety-five point something (cf. 95.675 according to an electronic calculator). It is evident that a high degree of precision to many decimal places is not possible in a single computation with a slide-rule, so computations would need to be split into different components and the results added together if great precision were needed.

Slide moved so that 1 on slide is adjacent to 21.5 on fixed scale

4.45 on sliding scale read off to find product on fixed scale

eager teenager, Blaise had applied his mind to the number of calculations his father had to carry out in the course of his duties. What was needed was a calculating machine, to automate the required addition and subtraction. Pascal started work in 1642. The device he created was effective and clever – indeed his dial-based technology persisted as a fundamental idea in adding machines right through to the development of electronic computers – but commercially unsuccessful. Gottfried Leibniz, the German co-inventor of calculus, had a similar idea and then heard about Pascal's machine. Leibniz's was more ambitious, since it would do all four basic arithmetical operations, but both inventors' concepts were doomed owing to the cost and unreliability of precision engineering before the development of modern mass-production machine tools.

PASCAL.

Engraved for the Encyclopedia Londinensis, 1811

Blaise Pascale's adding machine had wheels, each of which showed the numbers 0 to 9. To create an 'input', the wheel was

Blaise Pascal is best known as a mathematician and a theologian, but he made an important contribution to computing too.

Pascal's adding machine featured a system to 'carry' a digit by transferring a unit to the next wheel – an essential feature of all tallying machines.

rotated using a thin rod so that the desired input number was shown in a display window. To add a second number, that number was dialled, so that the sum would show in the display window. The clever part of the device is a system for 'carries' – that is, the transfer to the next wheel of a unit when the lower wheel has completed a whole revolution. A carry feature is essential to all counters and some variation of it can be found in machines used for keeping tally – such as odometers in cars and the turnstile-counting of football crowd size – into modern times.

Computing all at sea

These inventions seem largely to have been glamorous toys for the rich rather than workhorses for everyday computing. Most arithmetic was being done by hand, using pencil and paper. And there was lots of it. Not only did clerks in businesses and government have to write things out in ledgers and tot up columns of figures, but more complex calculations had increasingly found their way into everyday life. Possibly the most extreme example was navigation and, in particular, the problem of determining longitude at sea. To determine longitude (distance east or west from your starting point) there were various methods, but two stand out. The easiest one was to observe the sun at noon wherever the ship was located and compare this with the ship's master chronometer, which gave the precise time at the Greenwich

Meridian. A simple calculation converted the time difference into distance east or west of Greenwich. Only that was not so easy after all, since reliable chronometers were hard to come by and extremely expensive, even after John Harrison's invention of sea-going clocks over the period 1730–60. The other method was by lunar observations. These only required accurate observation while at sea and did not depend on reliable time-keeping instrumentation. But they did require a formidable amount of calculation, to convert a lunar observation into a position at sea; and it was just not feasible to expect

John Harrison was the first person to calculate longitude accurately while aboard ship in 1713. He built a working sea-going chronometer to measure time differences to help him solve this problem.

MARY EDWARDS

Mary Edwards was a computer. In 1773, her husband, John, a Church of England curate, was offered computing work for the Nautical Almanac. John was busy, not just looking after the souls of his parish but also brewing up chemicals and constructing telescopes, so he was disinclined to do the work of looking up logarithms and adding them and checking astronomical tables and recording the new data. Mary Croarken noted in her research that 'For each tabular entry calculated, the computer had to perform perhaps 12 table lookups and 14 seven- or eight-figure sexagesimal arithmetic operations.' This tedious work was left to Mary. She performed it quickly and accurately and when John died after inhaling too much arsenic in 1784 she worked directly for the Nautical Almanac in her own right. She carried on doing so, and checking other computers' work, continuously until 1811 and occasionally thereafter until her death in September 1815. The reason for her dedication was not so much enjoyment but the need for a steady source of income, especially after John's Church of England stipend ceased. She had children to bring up – one of whom, Eliza Edwards, also became a Nautical Almanac computer.

sea-captains to stop what they were doing and disappear into a cabin for hours each day to cover pages in figures, let alone risk an error in the mathematics. Some kind of shortcut was needed.

So the British Board of Longitude produced a Nautical Almanac, first published in 1767, under the direction of the Astronomer Royal, Nevil Maskelyne, which set out tables containing pre-calculated data that sailing-masters could readily consult to simplify the conversion of observations to information about position. Every year new tables had to be produced, looking forward for years to come given the duration of voyages at that time. To compile the tables, the Board hired computers to carry out the necessary predictive calculations.

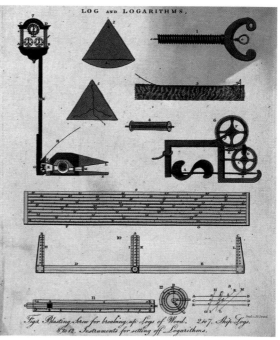

The various instruments depicted here were used to aid in the calculation of logarithms – work that could be tedious and time-consuming when done manually.

Tables of pre-computed data persisted into relatively modern times. Many readers will remember from their schooldays carrying booklets of tables to mathematics lessons. These booklets contained tables of logarithms, trigonometric functions, statistical data and more: all requiring someone to have computed the data accurately and transcribed it without typographical error into the tables. Books of tables were used by adults as well and not just in scientific and mathematical occupations.

Business users needed tables: in insurance, finance, government, construction and commerce.

Getting the tables done, and getting them done right, was tough, probably too tough for humans with low boredom thresholds and weak attention to detail. A complex society needed a more reliable solution. With the steam age, and the energetic approach to engineering that came with it, the mechanization of computing might just become a realistic possibility.

READY RECKONER

My father John (Alan Turing's brother) was a lawyer. When he packed up his office and retired in 1977, among his books was a small red item called a 'Ready Reckoner'. Its hundreds of pages consisted of tables of calculations, such as the return after so many years on a sum of £5,000 invested at a range of rates such as $3\frac{3}{8}\%$, $3\frac{1}{2}\%$, $3\frac{5}{8}\%$, $3\frac{3}{4}\%$ and so on. Such calculations were difficult, since the British had retained, until close to my father's retirement, the most obscure and difficult currency system, with 12 pence to the shilling and 20 shillings to the pound (or 21 shillings to the guinea – lawyers traditionally billed their clients in guineas). No wonder he needed help from the Ready Reckoner.

After decimalization, the office invested in a four-function electronic calculator, one of those desk models with huge buttons. Occasionally it was found in my father's office. The Ready Reckoner was placed on the shelf with the law books after that.

A four-function electronic calculator. This large, desk-bound machine was a relief to office workers across the world.

Chapter 2

COMPUTING WITH STEAM

Charles Babbage invented engines
to produce more accurate data than
contemporary tables of logarithms
contained. Machinery to do calculations
developed along with modernized
Victorian technology, drawing on the
tradition of machinery controlled by
punched cards. The culmination was
Herman Hollerith's counting and
tabulation machines originally devised
for processing the United States census
in 1890.

The industrial revolution brought with it a
fascination with steam power. Suddenly it seemed
that every human problem, even computing, could
be solved by the power of steam.

The problem with all those tables of figures was that they had been computed by people. Errors slipped in at every stage: in the computing, needless to say, but also in transcribing the computed numbers, in the typesetting, in the proof-reading … and this drove users of the tables to distraction. In 1821, the mathematician and engineer Charles Babbage was, together with his friend and fellow-scientist John Herschel, comparing two sets of tables prepared for the Astronomical Society. The two sets of figures had been computed independently and should have presented the same information, but there were errors – lots of them. Ultimately Babbage exclaimed: 'I wish to God these calculations had been executed by steam!'

Stephenson's Rocket transformed the nature of transport and led to the railway boom of the 19th century.

Nuts and bolts

It was the steam age and the reliability, power and automation of steam seemed to be the solution to many problems. If steam could provide solutions in the fields of flooded mine workings and ventilation, and even steam-powered locomotives were being tested, perhaps the new technology could also be applied to computation? In fact, the search for a solution that was tempting Babbage at this time had less to do with the source of power that steam offered, but the developments in mechanical engineering that went with it. While Watt and Trevithick and Stephenson had been evolving designs that

would lead to steam engines hauling trains along railways, the techniques for achieving manufactures had been changing too. Iron-casting was allowing for standardization and, with it, greater precision in the mass-production of identical parts. Screws and bolts were becoming available that would fit standard-sized, mechanically drilled bores. Machine-tools were becoming more sophisticated. What Babbage had really been talking about was mechanization of the computing process.

And Babbage, with his immense ability to turn his scientific mind to any project requiring imagination, persistence and

A steam-powered pump is used to irrigate a farmer's fields.

attention to detail, was now on the case. In fact, it seems that he had been thinking about mechanized computation for several years already, but now he was galvanized into motion. It occurred to Babbage that a machine could be constructed that would be perfectly capable of doing complex calculations, since many types of calculation can be approximated by a 'polynomial', that is a mathematical function in which the 'variable' (the unknown number you are trying to find – e.g. x) is positive and found by addition, subtraction, multiplication or division only. For example, $3x - x^2 + 5$ is a simple polynomial. School students will have encountered polynomials in quadratic equations (such as $2x^2 + 2x - 12 = 0$), but many more complex behaviours can be modelled with these functions.

Charles Babbage's insight was to exploit a feature of polynomials that enables them to be reduced by a series of steps to very simple additions, using the 'method of differences'. Babbage himself gave the example of a pile of cannon-balls heaped up in a triangular pyramid. The number of balls in each layer of the pyramid can be counted and the difference in the number of balls between each layer worked out and then the difference between the differences and so on.

Layer	Number of balls	Difference	2nd difference
Top	1		
		2	
2nd	3		1
		3	
3rd	6		1
		4	
4th	10		1
		5	
5th	15		1
		6	
Bottom	21		

FRENCH REVOLUTION

After 1789, France had a problem. Once the aristocrats had all been sent to the guillotine, the demand for coiffeurs tailed off. The hairdressers needed new jobs. The mathematician Gaspard Riche de Prony had an idea: he could deploy them as computers, provided he could find computing simple enough for a redundant prinker to do.

The answer to simplification was a pyramid. At the top, professional mathematicians. In the middle, people who split the problems into pieces for addition or subtraction. At the bottom, the hairdressers. It wasn't very *égal* but it gave them something to do. And the model inspired Babbage: at bottom, all his mechanized process needed to do was add or subtract.

The French Revolution had computing problems of its own. Professional mathematicians could no longer handle the sheer quantity of work required to solve their problems, so they found assistants who could handle smaller problems of addition and subtraction.

Using the 'method of differences', even quite complex functions can be reduced to a simple process of addition. To quote Babbage, 'from the preceding explanation, it appears that all Tables may be calculated, to a greater or less extent, by the method of Differences.'

All he needed to do now was to

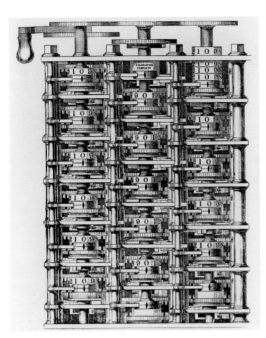

Charles Babbage's Difference Engine had people only input their problems and the machine would spit out an answer. Unlike previous machines, it did not require human supervision.

mechanize the idea, with or without the aid of steam. Babbage's idea was in keeping with the spirit of the times and with his influence he was able to procure funding from the British Government to bring it about. Within a remarkably short time, and with the assistance of his talented engineering colleague Joseph Clement, Babbage constructed a demonstration model of a Difference Engine that was exhibited in 1832. It was only able to compute functions to the third degree of difference, but the fact that it worked proved

Babbage's concept. The stage was set for the full-scale Difference Engine to be built and to solve the nation's problem of consistent computing.

The Difference Engine is worked by a crank. This is not an insult to the operator, nor is it another claim that Babbage was an obsessive sort of chap, but a description of the back-and-forth motion used to power the machine. The crank turns a shaft that has the appearance of a vertical steel axle carrying a number of discs, flattish cylinders with the figures 0 to 9 engraved around the edge, as on old-fashioned British pound coins where you could turn the coin sideways to read the words *Decus et Tutamen* (meaning 'ornament and security', a phrase Babbage might have deployed for his own device). The axle shows the number of units on the bottom disc, the tens on the next one, hundreds on the third disc up and so on.

If the Difference Engine is calculating a series of squares (4, 9, 16, 25, 36 …) this can be represented by a table of differences thus:

Results	1st difference	2nd difference
1		
	3	
4		2
	5	
9		2
	7	
16		2
	9	
25		2
	11	
36		

Charles Babbage was a British mathematician and is best known as the inventor of the computer. He was an eccentric figure who could be difficult to work with but he was a man of undeniable genius.

IRASCIBLE GENIUS

Charles Babbage was born in 1791. He was 'educated' at Cambridge, where he skipped lectures to go on outings because the teaching there in 1810 was unimpressive. What he achieved was to build up an impressive circle of influential people whom he charmed with his intellect, good looks and sense of fun. He could be opinionated, but robust debate was *de rigueur*. He wrote extensively, not just on mathematics but on economics and manufacturing, and attempted unsuccessfully to professionalize the Royal Society, which was becoming a den of patronage.

The first biography of Charles Babbage was written in 1964. His biographer described him as an 'irascible genius'. This may be fair; but the image of Babbage as a cantankerous old curmudgeon whose projects failed owing to his obstinacy and lack of diplomatic skills is almost certainly too simplistic. Some cameos from his life give a sense of the contradictions in this man:

1842: Prime Minister Sir Robert Peel wants to 'get rid of Mr Babbage and his calculating machine', or rather its cost, which is a drain on scarce Treasury resources. Babbage seeks an interview, which is at last granted. Oblivious of the political context, Babbage launches into a recitation of grievance about how much the Government *owes him*. Peel responds, with some justification, that by Babbage's own account an Analytical Engine (see opposite) renders the Difference Engine obsolete. Babbage storms out of the meeting.

1843: Ada Lovelace is trying to stop Babbage including a diatribe against the Government in her annotated description of the Analytical Engine. 'I have been harassed and puzzled in a most perplexing manner by the conduct of Mr. Babbage ... I am sorry to come to the conclusion that he is one of the most impracticable, selfish, and intemperate persons one can have to do with.'

1844: Bored with a performance of Mozart's *Don Giovanni*, Babbage goes back-stage, and quizzes the hands about the machinery. As the music grows to a crescendo – the Don is about to be swallowed by the demons of hell – Babbage sees a flash of lightning and a hole opening in the ceiling above him. Two irate devils jump at him, one on either side, and the floor on which they are standing begins to rise. To avoid tragedy becoming farce, the 53-year-old Babbage has to leap off the platform on to a narrow beam without colliding with the underside of the stage.

So, in order to calculate the squares, the Difference Engine needs to add 2 at the first column, a turn of the crank will cause 2 to be added to whatever number is showing on the second column (3), and then to add whatever that number is (now 5) to what is showing on the third column (4) to give the next result (9).

And the importance of the crank? It takes the human element out of the machine. Humans make mistakes, so the only points at which humans interfere are in setting up the problem to be computed and providing (in the absence of steam) a power source. This was unlike previous computing machines, which had needed humans to regulate the operations while the computing was going on. Automated computing had been born.

The large Difference Engine was never built. It's difficult, even with hindsight, to be certain what caused the project to run into the sand. But certain factors played a part: Babbage was busy on many projects; he wanted to improve the design; he was over-dependent on Joseph Clement to execute his designs and Clement's financial demands began to outstrip his output. Perhaps it was also because, in 1827, Babbage's son Charles died, followed only weeks later by his wife Georgiana. In any event by 1834 little progress had been made, there had been a change of government with the consequent loss of official support for the project and £17,478 14s 10d had been spent without any sign of development beyond the small demonstration model of 1832. To put this in perspective, this amount of cash would have bought 22 new Stephenson steam locomotives at 1831 prices.

Something analytical

By 1834 Babbage, whose mind was ever whirring with invention, had a new idea for the use of machinery in computation. The new idea was far more ambitious than the old Difference Engine: not only would it have all the capabilities of the Difference Engine, but it would be completely versatile. Babbage's new machine would have two extraordinary features that left the Difference Engine looking like so much scrap metal. First, it would be controllable – what, today, we would call programmable – so as to carry out whatever instructions were fed to it. Secondly, the machine would be capable of modifying the instructions given to it and thus able to change its function to fit the output of its first operations. The new machine was going to be called the Analytical Engine.

Charles Babbage was never daunted by a challenge, even a political one, and he exploited his connections with highly placed friends and his own soaring reputation to push ahead with the Analytical Engine. There would be a vast amount of research, as the capabilities required of the machine would go up to and beyond the limits of modern engineering and precision design.

Charles Babbage's Analytical Engine anticipates the modern computer in many respects. Although it was never built, the detailed drawings and descriptions that survive indicate the scheme of its design. As with the Difference Engine, there were to be columns of discs, each disc showing figures around the edges. Some of these columns showed the data being processed – in effect, these columns constitute a memory, or what Babbage called the machine's 'store'. The numbers showing on the columns in the

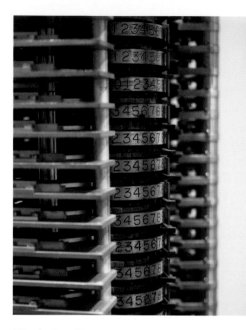

The Analytical Engine was Babbage's magnum opus, but a lack of funding and political support meant that it remained nothing more than an elaborate idea.

store could be transferred to other columns, allowing the data to be processed: the processing apparatus was called the 'mill'. The columns were disposed so that the mill could easily access the data in the store and return data to the store after completion of a process.

Unlike the Difference Engine, though, a variety of different processes would be possible. The operational behaviour of the mill was controlled through punched cards, as in the Jacquard loom (see opposite). So was the input of data into the store.

An example of a problem that the Analytical Engine could solve was set out in a paper written by Italian military engineer and mathematician Luigi Menabrea. The object is to compute the value of x in the simultaneous equations

$$mx + ny = d$$
$$m'x + n'y = d'$$

These equations can be rearranged (try dividing by n and n' respectively, subtract the second equation from the first and simplify) to get

$$x = (dn' - d'n)/(n'm - nm')$$

which is the equation the machine can solve, given values for m, n, d, m', n' and d'. The operations might look something like this, if the initial values are assigned to data-columns V_0 to V_5:

Number	Operation	Operands	Results stored at	Process of computation
1	×	$V_2 \times V_4$	$= V_8$	dn'
2	×	$V_5 \times V_1$	$= V_9$	$d'n$
3	×	$V_4 \times V_0$	$= V_{10}$	$n'm$
4	×	$V_1 \times V_3$	$= V_{11}$	nm'
5	−	$V_8 - V_9$	$= V_{12}$	$dn'-d'n$
6	−	$V_{10} - V_{11}$	$= V_{13}$	$n'm-nm'$
7	÷	$V_{12} \times V_{13}$	$= V_{14}$	X

The industrial revolution was all about textiles. Mechanization, in the form of spinning jennies and flying shuttles, was speeding up production through automation. Mechanization also stimulated the inventiveness of those who saw what machinery could do. As long ago as 1725, the silk-weavers of Lyon in France were trying to find ways to automate the tedious process by which patterns were woven into damask. In standard unpatterned cloth, the long threads (the warp) are raised alternately and the shuttle containing the transverse thread (the woof) is passed through after each alternation. To create a pattern or a more intricate design, the threads of the warp to be raised must be selected separately for each passage of the shuttle. Doing this by hand limited the creativity of the patterns, owing to the fiddliness of selecting the threads. Hooks were used to engage the threads to be lifted and the question was how to automate, or mechanize, the process of selection.

The Jacquard Loom, invented in 1801, used punched cards to instruct the loom to lift a hook or leave it in place, saving the operator countless hours of tedium.

Knockout punch

The automata of the mid-18th-century copied clockwork designs, whereby studs or perforations on a cylinder could repeat patterns. The silk weavers soon recognized that this idea could be adapted to control the behaviour of the hooks in a loom; the idea reached maturity with the invention of a fully-automatic patterning machine by Joseph-Marie Jacquard in 1801. His system used punched cards instead of punched paper, which had been used in predecessor designs. Each card represented one lift of the warp; each hook was engaged with its thread, or not, according to whether a hole was in the card. Instead of the operator having to reset the hooks for each run of the shuttle, it was simply a case of transferring a drawn pattern line-by-line into a set of punched cards, which would cycle through the machine mechanically. A portrait of Jacquard, woven on one of his looms, required 24,000 cards. What Jacquard had brought to automation was the ability to program – to select different

This portrait, woven by one of Jacquard's looms, required 24,000 punched cards to create.

behaviours according to the information on the card.

Babbage's extraordinary idea for an Analytical Engine could be brought to life if he could exploit the punched-card technology of the Jacquard process. Cards could be used to reconfigure the operational part of the machine – what he called the 'mill' – to adapt itself and carry out different tasks, just as in a Jacquard loom; and they could also be used in the same way to re-set the variables to be operated on, that is (as we might put it today) for data input. As with Jacquard's looms, rods would be activated or deactivated depending on the presence or absence of a hole in the cards and the rods would act on the parts of the machine containing or processing data. Cylinders, called 'barrels', would have protruding

CHIMING CLOCK

In the dining-room at home is an antique clock bought in about 1920 by my great-uncle Harvey. It was made by an English clockmaker during the reign of Charles II and it is older than anything else in the house. Although the clock is in perfect working order, it is not allowed to run, because of its chiming mechanism. As the clock winds around to strike the hour, a studded barrel starts to rotate. Studs on the barrel flick hammers that strike little bells and a tinny tune starts to play. Changing the positions of the studs changes the tune. This ancient mechanism shows how long ago it was possible to store a program, even though no one would confuse the dining-room clock with a computer. Alas, the musical chimes interfere with piano practice and so the clock is required to stay silent.

studs that encoded specific processes like addition. The Engine would be able to cycle through the same process iteratively, carry out separate processes in parallel, switch processes conditionally depending on the output of an earlier process, print its output or even produce its output in the form of punched cards (which could re-cycle as input) and more. And the machine would stop when it found a solution (or continue endlessly if the problem were not solvable).

All that sounded fantastical, or incomprehensible, to most people, for whom the steam-engine was the limit of what might be achieved with technology. Machines for computation were an idea only the most enthusiastic would embrace. Fortunately for Babbage, enthusiasts were around: most notably the amateur mathematician Ada

Byron, daughter of the poet Lord George Byron. Married at 20 to a man who became the Earl of Lovelace shortly afterwards, Ada, Countess of Lovelace, became a promoter and developer of Babbage's ideas. Having mastered the capabilities of the Analytical Engine, she is hailed as the author of some of the world's first software.

But the Analytical Engine was never built. The spirit of the times had changed – there would never be the flow of funds that had financed the Difference Engine project and Babbage's track-record for delivery was not good. Even so, it is arguable that Babbage never intended to *build* the Analytical Engine – his research was directed towards assessing its feasibility, recognizing that the demands it would make on precision

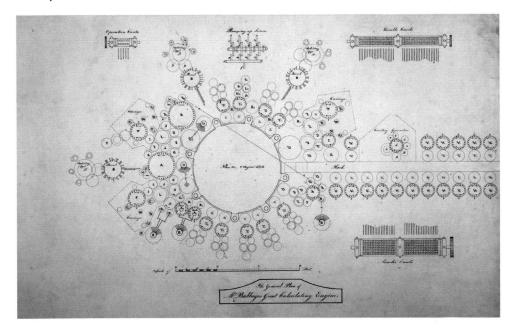

The Analytical Engine could be reprogrammed for different tasks and would continue its operation until it found a solution.

ADA, FIRST LADY OF SOFTWARE

Ada, Countess of Lovelace (1815–52), is the most romantic figure in the history of computing. The only legitimate child of the poet Lord Byron, she never actually knew her father, which may have contributed to the rather different direction her own intellectual life took. At about 18 years of age, she was introduced to Charles Babbage, beginning a working relationship that lasted until her death from cancer at the age of 36. Babbage, already 42 when they met, outlived her by 19 years.

Lovelace's personal contribution to computing was, principally, as interpreter of Babbage's ideas for an Analytical Engine. A description in French had been prepared by Luigi Menabrea, mathematician, military engineer and later prime minister of Italy; Lovelace translated the description for publication in Britain, but contributed seven 'notes' that add substantially to Menabrea's account. The 'notes' are about three times the length of the main text and spell out in much more detail what could in principle be done with the machine.

Ada Lovelace, the daughter of Lord Byron, worked closely with Babbage on the analytical engine and developed an algorithm for computing Bernoulli's numbers.

The most famous is Note G, which sets out an algorithm for computing Bernoulli's numbers. These are a sequence of rational numbers (that is, any number that can be expressed as a fraction – p/q – of two whole numbers) with deep connections to number theory. Not only does Note G break down the algorithm into steps, but its author explains what operational cards would be used to carry them out. Ada Lovelace is thus considered to be the first person to have written a computer program.

Lovelace also thought about a different kind of note. In Note A, Lovelace says that the Analytical Engine might 'act upon other things beside number' and she gives as an example that musical sounds might be 'susceptible of expression' within the notation of the machine, so that 'the engine might compose elaborate and scientific pieces of music'.

As was conventional, Lovelace signed her work with her initials, AAL. It is a sign of those times that her mathematical contemporaries found this an uncomputable puzzle: they knew of no mathematicians with those initials. No *male* mathematicians, that is.

machine technology were unprecedented. The intricate drawings that remain are a testament to what might – might – have been.

Taxing problems

Since earliest times, governments have needed to count people in order to tax them. We are informed that around the time of

REINVENTING THE WHEEL

Babbage's Analytical Engine foresaw a vast range of innovations that modern computer science takes for granted, but that were painstakingly worked out anew during the middle of the 20th century. These include the reduction of complex mathematical processes to atomized steps – the precise formulation of algorithms; the absence of human intervention during computation; computing as rules-based processing of symbols that are meaningless in themselves; the equivalence of variables and instructions as different forms of data; solvability defined by whether the machine halts; and even machines as 'thinking' artefacts. This is an impressive catalogue. One is therefore tempted to ask, 'How come it took till the 20th century to reinvent all these wheels? What went wrong?'

Sometimes the question is asked in a different way: 'Did Alan Turing know about Babbage and his work?' The answer is 'Probably not – at least until after his time at Bletchley Park.' There was a wealth of mathematical and engineering talent at Bletchley – someone there had heard of Babbage's work. But until then, knowledge of Babbage was something of a rarity. There was Lovelace's paper, the documents referred to in it, and Babbage's son Henry posthumously published the design drawings and other materials issued in 1889. But these were all specialist and obscure works, to be found by researchers in archives rather than out in the mainstream. Without Babbage to promote it, his work had disappeared under a pile of dust.

Babbage's work slowly began to come to light following publication of a Science Museum paper in 1933, but it is uncertain whether Alan Turing's attention had been drawn to it when he began thinking about computing and machinery in 1935. It's more likely that attention really began to focus on Babbage and his remarkable insights after the breakneck-speed developments in computing theory and machinery seen during the period 1935–50.

the birth of Christ, there went out a decree from Caesar Augustus that all the world should be taxed – and as our informant is St Luke, who was a tax-man, we can assume he is reliable. Taxation requires knowledge of the population and tax-gathering is closely connected with census-taking and the collection of statistics. Enlightened countries also need to understand their populations in order to regulate electoral processes.

Tax, democracy and statistics are all bound up together. In its original form, the Constitution of the United States specified, in article 1, section 2:

Representatives and direct Taxes shall be apportioned among the several States which may be included within this Union, according to their respective Numbers, which shall be determined by adding to the whole Number of free Persons, including those bound to Service for a Term of Years, and excluding Indians not taxed, three fifths of all other Persons. The actual Enumeration shall be made within three Years after the first Meeting of the Congress of the United States, and within every subsequent Term of ten Years, in such Manner as they shall by Law direct.

From as early as Caesar Augustus's times, governments have needed to tax their populations. Doing so required a detailed knowledge of the population, which could only be done by taking a census.

By the late 19th century the reference to 'free Persons' had been dropped, and the population had risen threefold to 63 million in the decade before 1890. However, taking the census using pen-and-paper manual methods was too slow: the next census was already being organized before the data from the last one had been collated and made available. A mechanized process was obviously needed, and in the United States there was no risk of scepticism or misplaced conservatism opposing such a development. On to the scene came Herman Hollerith, founder of what is now IBM, a man with a plan.

The census problem brought into focus a variety of types of computation needed: not only did things have to be counted, but they needed to be sorted and re-sorted and then the totals counted needed to be added (and occasionally subtracted) and then the output printed in neat tables. Tabulating machines were going to be complicated.

Technology for counting and adding was not really new; what Hollerith contributed was sorting. Hollerith's initial solutions for sorting were not particularly successful, but the central idea was sound. Punched-card technology not only allowed for data to be stored, one card per person in the population, but it also had an in-built system for automated selection, as in the Jacquard loom process. Provided that the tabulating machine could be programmed to choose which holes to select for, sorting could be mechanized. Programming was initially done through a plugboard, but in time Hollerith switched to a punched-card drive for sorting as well as data recording.

Ascent of the analogues

It was perhaps no coincidence that the success of Hollerith's company followed the injection of management talent that had been

Punched cards formed the 'software' for early computing machines. The holes punched in the cards formed the binary instructions necessary to tell the machine to follow one path or another.

BIRTH OF A GIANT

Herman Hollerith (1860–1929) graduated with a mining degree from Columbia University. 'Mining' was a code-word meaning engineering: Hollerith was first and foremost an inventor. His tabulating machine company targeted governments carrying out censuses, but had more limited success with the commercial sector. By 1911, a number of business problems – poor sales, badly co-ordinated production, weaknesses in technical development, a debt burden, confused post-merger corporate structure – were hindering its progress.

Thomas J. Watson (1874–1956) did not go to university, but attended a year's course in accounting and business in Elmira, New York. Watson held a number of jobs before joining the National Cash Register Company (NCR) in 1896. He soon excelled at sales and eventually became general sales manager. In 1914 he joined the Computing-Tabulating-Recording Company originally founded by Hollerith. Within four years its revenues had doubled. The company was renamed International Business Machines (IBM) in 1924 and the rest is history.

Herman Hollerith was an American inventor responsible for creating the tabulating machine that would prove essential to speeding up the process of census-taking.

Hollerith's tabulating machine used punched cards to help mechanize the sorting process.

developed in a cash-register company. Cash registers are a typical example of an office machine that had evolved from the simpler adding machines of a previous generation.

Moreover, as society and technology developed, the types of calculation needed had become more complicated. While mechanical adding machines and slide-rules might be used for complex formulae, the time required could be excessive and the precision of slide-rules was poor. Specialist machines were invented to fill the gaps and speed up computations. Mechanical devices of increasing ingenuity assisted computational processes.

ADDING MACHINE

Adding machines persisted well into the 20th century, being superseded only by cheap electronic calculators, which came on to the market in the mid-1970s. Until then, offices had depended for everyday calculations on adding machines such as the Brunsviga. Dozens of manufacturers produced dozens of models, with many complex and intriguing design elements that distinguished them from their competitors' inventions.

In any such machine, a figure to be added is transmitted to an 'accumulator' by means of a gear or similar device. For example, you might need to add 4,992 to 17,305. The first step would be to key in the first number and usually you would turn a crank to rotate cog-wheels inside the machine that moved an amount of angular distance corresponding to the numbers selected. The movement of the crank caused wheels in the accumulator to rotate; in many models, the number in the accumulator could be seen by looking through a window at a register. Once the crank had turned, the keys were reset, allowing a second

The Brunsviga machine was a mechanical adding machine that relied on turning a crank to rotate its cog-wheels to find out the answer.

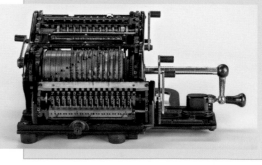

number to be keyed in. The crank was turned again, adding the new number to the accumulator.

A challenge is the stepping mechanism, which is needed for 'carries' when the number of units exceeds 9 on any wheel. A typical way of achieving this is to use the ratchet-and-pawl system of counters.

Decimal digits								
1	2	3	4	5	6	7	8	9
⊛	⊛	⊛	⊛	⊛	⊛	⊛	⊛	⊛
Complements								
8	7	6	5	4	3	2	1	0
⊛	⊛	⊛	⊛	⊛	⊛	⊛	⊛	⊛

Much more troublesome is machinery for subtraction. Most machines used the 'method of complements'. Each number from 0 to 9 has a complementary number: the complement is what you would need to add to get to nine: $1 + 8 = 9$, $2 + 7 = 9$, $3 + 6 = 9$ and so forth. Having found the complement of the number to be subtracted (in the example given below, $9999 - 6608$ gives the complement 3391) you then add it to the larger number you are subtracting from ($7402 + 3391$ to give 10793). This is the balance, once you make two adjustments: discard the 1 at the beginning of the sum and add 1 to the units column; for example:

Conventional arthithmetic	Complements method		
	First, find complement of 6608	Next, add the complement	Finally, move the '1'
7402 − 6608 expected answer: 794	→ complement 3391	7402 + 3391 10793	adjust ones: 0794

Adding machines sometimes put the complements on their keys as well, in a different type, for when the machine was to be used for subtraction. The complements in the units column were one higher (treating the complements of units as $1 \equiv 9$, $2 \equiv 8$ and so on) so the operator did not have to remember to add one to get the correct balance.

Modern digital computers, using binary arithmetic, can subtract using a complement-of-two approach.

Perhaps the most complicated type of analogue computing device was the differential analyser. Differential analysers depended on rotating-plate-and-friction-wheel technology to extract information about the behaviour of troublesome mathematical functions. The machines themselves could be assembled very simply – Professor Douglas Hartree built one out of Meccano at Manchester in 1934 – although the equations they were used to solve could be highly involved. One attraction of differential analysers was that some degree of feedback could be used, with outputs from one part of the machine being used as input for another.

Consul the Educated Monkey was a calculating tool designed in 1915 to help children with multiplication.

What	How it works	Examples	Example of use
Counter *pawl and ratchet*	To move the 'tens' wheel on one place for every complete rotation of the 'units' wheel, a pawl engages with a ratchet	Elm City Counter	turnstile
Adder *pulleys*	A rope makes a half-turn around a pulley wheel. Hauling in *x* metres of rope on one side, then *y* metres on the other, causes the pulley to move up by ½ $(x + y)$	Kelvin tide predictor	tide prediction
Multiplier *bar-linkage*	Rigid bars are joined by pivots and constrained by slides. Mathematical equations like the sine function, multiplication, and the generation of logarithms can be modelled according to the orientation, length and hingeing of the bars	Consul, the educated monkey	torpedo aimer
Integrator (usually called a 'differential analyser') *friction wheels*	At right-angles to the surface of a spinning plate sits a small wheel. The further away the wheel is from the centre of the plate, the faster it rotates. The total angular movement *z* of the small wheel represents the integral of the distance *y* from the centre of the plate: $\Delta z = \frac{1}{r} y \Delta x$, or $z = \frac{1}{r} \int y dx$, where *r* is the radius of the small wheel	Wetli disk	determine cooling of poured steel

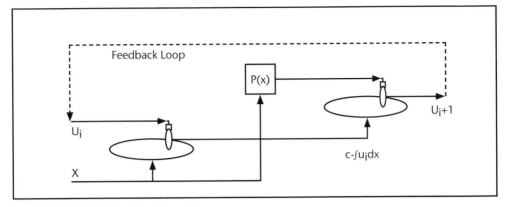

Differential analyzers coupled rotating discs to model mathematical functions. For some types of equation, the rotation of a small wheel, mounted perpendicularly and driven by a wide rotating disc, could be used to drive another disc, with its own output fed back to improve the accuracy of the first wheel's output.

One has to admire the inventiveness of these devices and the precision needed to bring them into being. But, from our own convenient perspective, it is easy to see that all the effort involved in creating a dedicated machine for a single type of problem could be disproportionate to the problem in question. What would be more efficient would be a programmable machine, like Hollerith's punched-card processors, which could be adapted to different tasks according to the user's needs.

Putting the spark into computing

The great innovation in Hollerith's punched-card machinery was the use of electricity. If steam was the transformative medium of the 18th century, surely electricity had a similar place in the 19th. As the century drew towards its close, readily available electricity could be used both as power source and as an integral part of the computation process. Hollerith's innovation was to use tiny cups of mercury and metal needles. Wherever there was a hole in one of his punched cards, the needle would dip into the mercury and make an electrical contact and this determined the sorting behaviour of the machine. Electricity was being used to make choices, decisions. Electricity was binary – on/off – and this new usage of the medium indicated the way forward for the new century.

So what point had computing reached, after the hectic second half of the 19th century? The innovations of that era had given the world programming and data storage. It was recognized that data-entry, data-output and program-entry could use the same type of input and as a result it was possible to have self-modifying programs. The Victorians had begun to use electricity, but were still dependent on physically moving machinery to execute processes: the primary use of electricity was still for power, not computation. It would take a new era and a world war to see the real potential of electric potential.

But before electricity could make a difference, what was needed was a theory of computing.

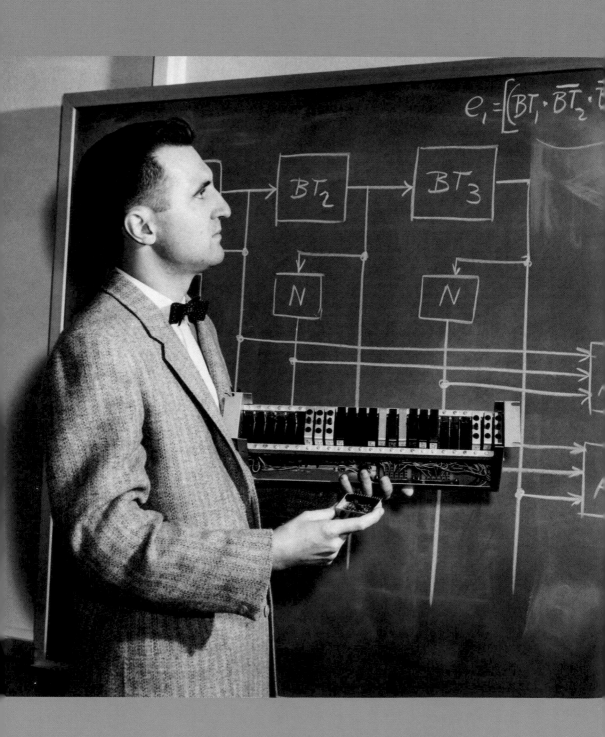

Chapter 3

LOGICAL DECISIONS

Mathematical approaches to logic began to shape computing. George Boole created a symbolic system for writing down propositions and deducing others from them. In the early 20th century, attempts were made to distil the whole of mathematics into computable symbols, but Kurt Gödel and Alan Turing showed that there were fundamental limits to this. Turing defined a model of a 'universal' computing machine in his paper on computable propositions; and it also became apparent that electrical circuits would behave logically according to Boole's system.

Logic was at the core of computing. Finding an effective way of expressing logical concepts, and even more importantly, placing them into a language that a machine could understand, was the key problem that occupied the mathematicians and philosophers of the early 20th century.

Computing reached a crossroads in the middle of the 20th century. So far, we have followed one path to that crossroads: the road characterized by the use of machinery and mechanical devices to assist with complex computations. Taking a different course, another road led to the junction: the road of mathematical logic.

What the human computers of the 19th century had been striving for was accuracy in their computing. However, the search for accuracy is not completely self-evident. What defines something as being the 'right' answer? If the purpose of computing is to achieve the objective of a correct answer, how will a human computer know that she has attained the goal? The reason we are doing complex computations is precisely that we do not know the answer and so have nothing to check it against. What is 103843884563 + 3368432099? Quick now and make no mistakes!

Doing the thing right

What the spirit of enquiry suggests is that a philosophy of computing might be needed. Computing involves processes and those processes ought to follow specific rules. So we need to know what the rules are in order to test whether a new method to assist with computing is valid. This body of knowledge – the philosophy of computing – is the study of logic: the deduction from first principles of unassailable conclusions.

As with mathematics, the study of logic can be traced back to the ancient Greeks. However, their approach to logic was largely based on use of language. A mathematical approach to logic began to emerge much later and is usually attributed to the work

The ancient Greek philosophers were the first to engage with the challenges of logic. Aristotle's conception of logic had an exceptional influence on Western thought.

of George Boole. Unlike the ancient Greek approach to logic, the Boolean approach was to take the elastic, malleable words out of the equation and replace them with neat, rigid symbols.

George Boole was a self-taught mathematician who rose from being a town schoolmaster to become Professor of Mathematics at Queen's College, Cork. His seminal work, *An Investigation of the Laws of Thought on which are founded the Mathematical Theories of Logic and Probabilities*, was published in 1853. Boole distilled the essence out of propositions and worked out an 'algebra' with which they

LANGUAGE, TRUTH AND LOGIC

Logic, as envisaged by Aristotle, was about the robustness of an argument and therefore about the study of what can legitimately be inferred from what. To put it another way, it is about language.

The English philosopher Alfred Jules ('A.J.') Ayer might have found it surprising that his name crops up in a book about computing. Ayer's line of study could not have been more different from that of the scientists, engineers and mathematicians whose stories make up much of this narrative. His book *Language, Truth and Logic* exposes the weaknesses of language as a medium for philosophy and deductive reasoning. Logic requires a firm root in observation and anything that does not follow from that is meaningless. Words that imply value judgments, such as 'justice', are vulnerable to the same attack. Ayer's book, written when he was only

The English philosopher A.J. Ayer concluded that language was unsuitable for expressing logical problems.

26, is combative, acid and trenchant and it came out in the same year as Alan Turing's paper 'On Computable Numbers' (see page 61). Both of them were appealing for a digital approach to seeking the truth.

could be combined without the need for verbiage: he thus founded the discipline of Symbolic Logic.

If propositions can be distilled into symbolic form and then combined and manipulated, that sounds very like what we do in simple arithmetic, by adding or multiplying. The rules may be different but the processes can be defined; and if the processes of simple arithmetic can be mechanized – as in Pascal's calculator or Babbage's Difference Engine – why could not the logical processes defined by Boole similarly be mechanized?

George Boole (1815–64) invented a symbolic language, an 'algebra' that could do without words.

BARBARA

The old logicians had identified four types of proposition:

- all *As* are *B* (all flies are insects) – type A
- no *As* are *B* (no flies are two-legged) – type E
- some *As* are *B* (some flies are green) – type I
- some *As* are not *B* (some flies are not annoying) – type O

and they devised mnemonics to help them remember which types of proposition can be validly (logically) grouped together. The mnemonic is a name comprising three syllables, with the vowels chosen from the list of types. The basic form of syllogism was called 'Barbara' (vowels AAA), which would give rise to simple syllogisms such as this:

- all wasps are insects (A)
- all insects are scary (A)
- all wasps are scary (A).

The other names for logically allowed combinations are so bizarre (Darapti, Felapton, Celarent, Bamalip and so on) that one wonders how they were a memory-aid at all.

In George Boole's symbolic approach to logic, '*P* and *Q*' is written as *PQ*, and '*P* or *Q* but not both' is written as *P* + *Q*. The exclusive form of 'or' is useful when thinking about mutually exclusive categories, such as (usually) male and female. Thus, in Boole's notation, a thing that is both *P* and *Q* – such as a monster (*P*) that has a scaly skin (*Q*) – is written as *PQ*, so a type A proposition would be expressed as $X = XY$. Which is not to say that all monsters have scaly skins.

Indeed they could. In the late 1860s, William Stanley Jevons devised and built a machine that would make deductions from propositions. He called it the 'logical abacus' but it looked like a piano, because it had a piano's characteristic upright shape and a keyboard. Most of the keys are labelled with letters, uppercase A representing proposition A and lowercase a representing the opposite (not-A), with the machine able to handle a total of four propositions. The other keys represent operations that can be carried out: there is a 'full-stop' key that

The keys of William Stanley Jevons's logic piano were labelled with upper- and lowercase letters that represented logical propositions.

corresponds to the 'enter' key on a modern computer keyboard, which you press to set the logic in motion, and there is one for clearing the machine before tackling the next problem. Once all propositions have been entered, the mechanism weeds out all except the allowable combinations, which are then shown on its face.

To show how Jevons's machine worked, imagine we have four ideas, such as:

- A: horses; a: non-horses
- B: mammals; b: non-mammals
- C: animals; c: non-animals
- D: Chinese things; d: things which are not Chinese.

We can see that some logical conclusions follow, such as 'all horses are mammals', which in Jevons's notation would be written as A = AB. If we input this, together with the other observation that all mammals are animals (B = BC) into the machine, it would tell us which combinations are allowed, thus:

- ABCD: Chinese horses
- ABCd: non-Chinese horses, so, for example, Ethiopian horses
- aBCD: Chinese cows,

and so forth, leading us to an understanding that Chinese frogs and Ethiopian rice-plants are possible, but you will never find a Chinese horse that is not a mammal.

W.S. Jevons (1835–82) had a wide variety of interests, including chemistry, politics, geometry, economics and logic. He also kept an extensive diary and his skill as

William Stanley Jevons (1835–82) had an astounding range of interests, including economics, logic, chemistry and even photography.

a photographer provides an extraordinary insight into the conditions of life in Australia, where he lived during his early career.

Jevons is remembered chiefly for his work in economics. His work on coal led to the 'Jevons paradox', which shows that as energy production becomes more efficient, consumption actually rises, contrary to what might be expected. Jevons's influence in logic and cryptology is less well-known but every bit as important. As well as devising the logic piano, his thinking about asymmetry in mathematical problems laid the foundations of modern cryptology. In his book *The Principles of Science* he describes asymmetric problems: those where it is easy to verify a solution, but extremely

ALICE

Lewis Carroll, whose reputation as a children's author has outlived his achievements as a mathematician, liked the idea of symbolic logic.

The Mock Turtle said that the four branches of arithmetic are ambition, distraction, uglification and derision. *Alice's Adventures in Wonderland* and its companion piece *Alice Through the Looking-Glass* are masterpieces in the literature of the absurd because logic is turned upside-down. Lewis Carroll also wrote a third book for children, called *The Game of Logic*, but it's not as famous, because it's really not much fun. Illogically, what is lots of fun is his serious book called *Symbolic Logic*, which has silliness among the syllogisms. Take this: All babies are illogical. Nobody is despised who can manage a crocodile. Illogical persons are despised. Conclusion: if you can manage a crocodile, you're not a baby. Or this: No kitten that loves fish is unteachable. No kitten without a tail will play with a gorilla. Kittens with whiskers always love fish. No teachable kitten has green eyes. No kittens have tails unless they have whiskers. Conclusion: Mr C.L. Dodgson was a bit bonkers, but great fun if you were called Alice Liddell and your father was busy writing a Greek dictionary.

Lewis Carroll's 'Alice' is one of the most endearing characters in children's fiction. Less well known, and less entertaining, is his final book for children, The Game of Logic.

hard to find it, a characteristic that recurs throughout this book.

Jevons is said to have enjoyed music as a recreation, but his qualities as a pianist are, unaccountably, not included in the historical record.

The ideas in Jevons's piano were reborn in the middle of the 20th century, when Wolfe Mays and Dietrich Prinz built an electromechanical logic machine out of spare bits and pieces culled from the Royal Air Force. It was called a Logical Computer. Its function was much the same as that of Jevons's device; its significance is that

*Here Dietrich Prinz, who built a 'logical computer',
sets a chess problem for a Ferranti computer.*

Prinz went on to become a pioneer in
programming and artificial intelligence.

Mechanizing logic does not take us any
closer to the fundamental question that
began this chapter: how would we know
what constitutes a valid set of rules? To
illustrate the problem, consider the worlds
of geometry. All students of Euclidean
geometry know that two parallel lines
never meet. This is a fundamental rule,
an axiom, of geometry. So it is presumably
absurd to suggest that there could be an
alternative universe in which parallel lines
might meet. Unfortunately, if you meet a
sea-captain, you will be swiftly disabused
of your narrow-minded preconceptions.

On the surface of the earth, lines
heading north and south appear
on the surface to be parallel, but
eventually they do meet. Euclidean
axioms need to be rewritten for
navigators. Navigation works, it's
just that the rulebook is different.

Rules about rules

By the start of the 20th century,
mathematicians had begun to look
behind the rules to enquire about
the rules for writing rulebooks.
Thinking crystallized into a set of
questions posed by the German
mathematician David Hilbert
in 1900. A set of constitutional
rules was needed, under which the
laws of any mathematical system,
such as Euclidean geometry, or
spherical geometry or arithmetic,
can be judged to be valid or invalid by
a mathematical version of the Supreme
Court. Hilbert proposed that validity would
exist where the system – the axioms and the
logical processes applied to make deductions
from them – satisfied three conditions:

• Consistency. For any given proposition,
once it's proved then that is final. You
should not be able to prove the contrary
by applying the rules in a different way.
In other words, no situation where two
courts looking at the same facts can reach
different verdicts.

• Completeness. All propositions could be
validly proved or disproved. None of that
woolliness that prevails in the civil courts,
which tolerate the idea that we don't
know but we'll decide something on the
balance of probabilities.

RUNNING MAN

Alan Mathison Turing OBE FRS (1912–54) is now a household name, but it was not always so. Until the revelations, from the late 1970s onwards, that the Government Code and Cypher School at Bletchley Park had read enemy coded messages during the whole of World War II and that Alan Turing had played an important role in that effort, knowledge of Alan Turing and his work was confined to the academic disciplines of pure mathematics and computer science.

Turing's life was short but packed with incident and discovery. His parents worked for the Indian Civil Service – that is, they were British expatriates who administered colonial India. Alan's childhood years were spent living with a foster-family while his real parents came home to Britain only for occasional holidays. Boarding school followed, where Alan quickly showed more interest in science and mathematics than in sport and classics (the subjects that young trainees for colonial administration were expected to master). He went on to King's College, Cambridge, to study mathematics, where he also discovered an enthusiasm for sports after all (he joined the rowing team at King's) and that it was not always necessary to conceal his homosexuality.

Alan Turing has become a household name in recent years. His efforts in decrypting the Enigma cipher earned him lasting recognition, but it only came decades after his death when the work of Bletchley Park was declassified.

After his success with the paper 'On Computable Numbers' he spent two years in the United States, returning just before the outbreak of World War II and in time to be recruited for Bletchley Park as a

King's College Cambridge fostered many great codebreakers, including Alan Turing.

specialist in the Enigma problem. After the war, he devoted several years to the design of computing machinery and by the end of his life his professional interest had moved into a completely new field, the study of shapes and forms of living things. Meanwhile he had also found time to develop his athletic abilities, reaching national standard in middle- and long-distance running, only narrowly missing being included in the 1948 Olympic squad.

However, Alan's sexuality marked him out and probably served to truncate his life. In early 1952, Alan Turing was convicted of 'gross indecency' – having gay relations with another man in Alan's house – and instead of being sent to prison or fined he was given the option of undergoing 'treatment' that took the form of a synthetic hormone implant, the purpose of which was to suppress his libido. Although Alan seemed to have recovered from the side-effects, both physical and mental, from this judicial form of torture, all was not entirely well and Alan Turing committed suicide a few days before his 42nd birthday in 1954.

Nowadays the idea that someone of his achievements and contribution to national survival could have been so treated seems absurd and repugnant. The British government issued an apology followed a few years later by a Royal Pardon. Recognizing that it was discriminatory to pardon one person, on the basis of achievements, rather than all those similarly convicted, a further more general pardon followed by Act of Parliament in 2017.

He never actually built such a Turing Machine as specified in 'On Computable Numbers' – indeed his concept of a machine was put forward to explore the idea of computable (and uncomputable) numbers. But Alan Turing liked machinery. He built a mechanical multiplier in Princeton, shortly after the 'On Computable Numbers' paper was published, and began work on an analogue machine designed to find solutions to the Riemann zeta-function. After the outbreak of the Second World War, his ability to think in mechanical terms was of invaluable assistance in helping solve the code-breaking problems that he was working on then. And that led to the development of a new generation of computing machines.

Alan Turing was an exceptional athlete as well as an eccentric genius. He came close to making Great Britain's 1948 Olympic squad for long-distance running.

CHAPTER 3

The German mathematician David Hilbert proposed that three elements were needed for valid rules: consistency, completeness and decidability.

be proved to be 'consistent'. Hilbert's first two constitutional ideas had been destroyed.

Gödel's approach to destroying Hilbert's program is interesting because he used the ideas of symbolic logic that had started with George Boole. Once you accept that mathematical propositions and processes can be precisely described in symbols, it follows that the symbols representing a process could be manipulated and processed just like any other data. In modern words, nothing fundamental distinguishes the data from the program – they are both strings of symbols. Gödel used the idea that the process is itself a piece of data to show that contradictions and paradoxes must exist, even in purely abstract mathematical systems. Just like the ancient Greeks there will be unhappy propositions such as 'Epimenides the Cretan says that all Cretans are liars', which can neither be proved nor disproved.

- Decidability. There is a general procedure to determine whether a proposition can be proved. Again, unlike the real messy world of litigation, in mathematics there should be some sort of infallible pretrial review process that can be used by the court to be sure that a verdict will be reached: no hung juries followed by retrials.

The question was, could anyone show that the rules of mathematics would obey these simple constitutional ideas? They became known as Hilbert's 'program'.

An Austrian mathematician, Kurt Gödel, working on Hilbert's 'program' showed, first, that ordinary arithmetic may not always be 'complete', and secondly, that it cannot

The Entscheidungsproblem

In 1935, in a classroom in Cambridge, a bespectacled young mathematics lecturer called Max Newman was explaining the Hilbert construct – or rather what remained of it – to a small group of students. In his class was an untidy graduate of King's

College called Alan Turing. Only the post-graduate students got to attend Newman's course because the idea that mathematics rested on shaky foundations might be too unsettling. In later life, Newman explained Hilbert's third proposition in terms of a 'mechanical process' for testing the provability of theorems.

Turing took Newman at his word. In a few feverish weeks, Turing had come up with a new concept that not only showed there was no litmus test for the provability of theorems – thus destroying any remaining crumbs of Hilbert's program for the laws of mathematics – but also put forward an entire theory of computing. Turing's paper, which being the output of a mere student languished on Newman's desk for a while, was called 'On Computable Numbers, with an application to the *Entscheidungsproblem*' (German for 'decision problem' as defined by David Hilbert in 1928). Turing only gets to the decidability question (the

Entscheidungsproblem) in section 11 – the very last one – of his paper, because the rest of it is concerned with a far more fundamental question: what, exactly, is it possible to compute? And what do we mean by 'computing'?

The key to what it can do is not in the complexity of its structure – it is so simple that it takes only a few lines to describe – but in the instructions that the machine must carry out (erase, print, shift tape) in light of what it scans. The instructions typically say: if the scanned symbol is this, do that. It's a logical, mechanical process. And it can carry out any computation – indeed what it can and cannot do is the very essence of computation. A 'universal' Turing machine can be programmed to behave like any other Turing machine described on the tape.

Alan Turing's concept of a simple machine was used, over the course of the rest of his paper on computable numbers,

In his famous paper, On Computable Numbers, Turing described a computing machine:

The 'computable' numbers may be described briefly as the real numbers whose expressions as a decimal are calculable by finite means ... According to my definition, a number is computable if its decimal can be written down by a machine...

We may compare a man in the process of computing a real number to a machine which is only capable of a finite number of conditions ... The machine is supplied with a 'tape' (the analogue of paper) running through it, and divided into sections (called 'squares') each capable of bearing a 'symbol'. At any moment there is just one square ... which is 'in the machine'. We may call this square the 'scanned square'. The symbol on the scanned square may be called the 'scanned symbol'. The 'scanned symbol' is the only one of which the machine is, so to speak, 'directly aware' ... In some of the configurations in which the scanned square is blank (i.e. bears no symbol) the machine writes down a new symbol on the scanned square: in other configurations it erases the scanned symbol. The machine may also change the square which is being scanned, but only by shifting it one place to right or left.

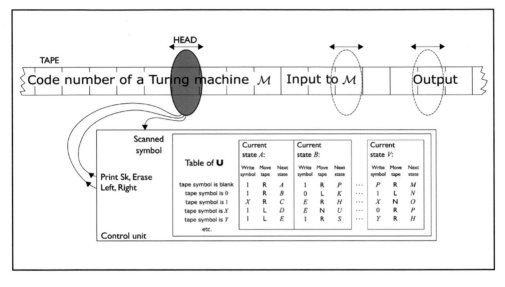

The idea of a 'Turing Machine' was set out in the 1932 paper 'On Computable Numbers'. The concept involved a simple, programmable machine that could solve almost any problem when provided with a few basic instructions.

to demonstrate through the advanced application of symbolic logic that functions exist which cannot be computed. He goes on to describe machines that go into an infinite loop ('circular machines'), thus setting up a challenge now known as the Halting Problem, or to put it crudely, whether you can devise a program to see if a program you just wrote will crash (in fact, as proved by Turing, you can't).

The significance of Alan Turing's paper was immediately noted in the world of mathematics, where the destruction of the final element of Hilbert's program was a significant development, but also because inadvertently Alan Turing had founded an entirely new field of mathematical study, that of computability.

In the longer term, the implications were quite different. Alan Turing's idea of a machine that acted on the basis of a table of instructions, the fact that the instructions could be read off the tape (the program is just so much data) to control the behaviour of the machine and the fact that the machine was digital in its operation laid a theoretical basis for all computers.

Binary thinking

In tackling an abstract question in symbolic logic, Alan Turing had come up with an imaginary machine. The idea of the universal machine was a rebirth of Charles Babbage's programmable, but unrealized, Analytical Engine. The idea of a machine that could be reset to do different things by giving it different instructions was still beyond the capabilities of modern engineering – or so it seemed. In 1937, at least three groups of American scientists began to use electricity in a binary way, which would fundamentally change the approach to automated computing.

Electricity is not self-evidently binary. You can vary the voltage as much as you want, subject to the limits imposed by the power-source available; indeed many

P AND NP

Polynomials (see page 33) have an important role in computing. They are very versatile: polynomial expansions can be used to approximate trigonometric functions like $\sin(x)$ and $\cos(x)$, π, find square roots and so on. Some of this was known to the Babylonians.

This is all fine and interesting enough and the foundation of versatility in Babbage's Difference Engine. Yet polynomials have continued to fascinate computer scientists. One challenge associated with computability is the amount of time it might take to solve a computable problem. An acceptable amount of time is defined by reference to whether it is 'polynomial time', in other words whether there is a polynomial function that can be applied to the thing you are trying to solve, expressing the amount of time needed to solve the problem.

An unacceptable alternative to 'polynomial time' might be 'exponential time'. Say your input is n:

• Fast problem: number of steps to solve might be in the order of n^2 or n^3 (a polynomial, then).
• Slow problem: number of steps to solve might be in the order of k^n (an exponential value).

To put some numbers on it, arbitrarily take three values of n and say that k is 2:

	$n=10$	$n=100$	$n=1000$
Polynomial (n^2)	100 steps	10,000 steps	1,000,000 steps
Exponential (2^n)	1,024 steps	1.26×10^{30} steps	1.07×10^{301} steps

So, if a problem can be solved in polynomial time, computability experts say it falls into the 'P' class; and if we don't know of an algorithm for solving it in polynomial time, it falls into the 'NP' class. A simple example of an NP problem is this: from the numbers -10, -3, -2, 7, 14 and 15, can you take a selection that together adds up to zero? It's simple to check that

$$-10 + -3 + -2 + 15 = 0,$$

so the answer is yes. But nobody has yet devised an algorithm that is not quantified in exponential time to *find* such an answer, so it's not clear that the problem belongs to the P class. An unsolved problem in computability theory is whether all NP problems are in the P class. It's not just mathematicians that care about this, or even computer scientists wondering how large the next super-computer needs to be. Everyday secure communication, such as sending credit card numbers over the Internet, depends on the existence of NP problems. How odd that we should actually crave problems too hard to be computed.

to logic, and binary arithmetic: computing, being a matter of right and wrong, should be digital.

All that remained to be done was to devise circuitry – or, if you prefer, logical processes – to carry out arithmetical operations and you would then have an electrical calculator that could do the same job as adding machines but more accurately and a lot faster. Electric currents can operate electromagnets and thereby open and close switches. Electromagnetic switches formed of relays were in common use in automated telephone exchanges before World War II and the technology was readily adapted to carry out 'if/then' logical functions. It was then a matter of devising switching systems and circuits that could tackle arithmetic.

In 1937, in another development in that breakthrough year, a Master's degree student at the Massachusetts Institute of Technology (MIT) called Claude Shannon saw that the behaviour of electrical circuits – the digital behaviour of combinations of switches, to be precise – exactly followed the logic that made up Boolean algebra. Shannon went on to use Boolean algebra to show how complex circuits could be simplified and how a circuit could be designed to model arithmetical operations and algebraic functions.

The use of electric current meant a binary approach to computing that fits perfectly with 'if A do B' type instructions.

computing machines developed during the 20th century that relied on electricity were analogue machines that exploited this variability. But the American developers had each, in different ways, recognized that electrical circuits use switching, which is exactly what instructions of the form 'if A then do B' require – the kind of instructions that Alan Turing had in mind for his imaginary machine. And once that connection had been made, the way was open to design circuits to achieve arithmetical operations, provided that one is willing to work in the base-2, or binary, system. There is a neat parity between truth tables, encountered in Boole's approach

TRUTH IS BINARY

Some of the time, truth is binary. If we set on one side the idea that some numbers are not actually computable, we can see an attractive symmetry between Boole's approach to dealing with logic and the binary system for dealing with arithmetic.

Boolean logic can be rendered in the form of truth tables. Keeping with the propositions
- some cats are black (x)
- some cats have stripes (y)

we can link the propositions in various ways:

AND ($\wedge$) – when both propositions are true

OR ($\vee$) – when either or both proposition is true

NOT ($\neg$) – when neither proposition is true

XOR ($\oplus$) – when either one is true, but not both

and create 'truth tables' that set out, in abbreviated form, what happens when the propositions are linked:

x	y	$x \wedge y$	Interpretation
T	T	T	cats that are black and striped, but not other types of cat (snow tiger)
T	F	F	
F	T	F	
F	F	F	

x	y	$x \oplus y$	Interpretation
T	T	F	cats that are black, but not striped, and cats that are striped, but not black, but no others ('exclusive or') (panthers and Bengal tigers)
T	F	T	
F	T	T	
F	F	F	

x	$\neg x$	Interpretation
T	T	cats that are not black (leopards)
F	F	

x	y	$x \vee y$	Interpretation
T	T	T	cats that are black or striped or both, but not cats that are neither ('inclusive or', more familiarly called 'and/or') (certainly not lions)
T	F	T	
F	T	T	
F	F	F	

Some of these tables are suspiciously familiar to arithmetical tables in a binary numerical system:

x	y	$x^x y$	Interpretation
1	1	1	multiplication and carry digit in addition
1	0	0	
0	1	0	
0	0	0	

x	y	$x + y$	Interpretation
1	1	0	modular addition (ignoring the carry, since 1 + 1 = 10 in binary)
1	0	1	
0	1	1	
0	0	0	

CARRY ON

Doing addition of binary numbers is challenging, because of the carry. In binary $1 + 1 = 10$ and that's a problem. First, Boolean algebra doesn't seem to handle the 1 to be carried into the twos column and secondly you need to deploy a larger number of digits in the sum than you had in the two starting-numbers.

The first problem is that the Boolean XOR operator adds $0 + 0$, $0 + 1$ and $1 + 0$ nicely but gives the result 0 if you try to add $1 + 1$: the carry digit gets lost. However, if you had used the Boolean AND operator, you would have got the answer 1 only if you were adding $1 + 1$ and not in any other situation. Combining the two operations sorts it out: XOR for the units column and AND for the carry, and now you have the right answer.

The second problem is well known to electronics engineers as the overflow problem. Arithmetic can go badly wrong if the numbers to be added are large: if the number of bits allocated to the problem is too small, the most significant digits can get lost. For example, if we wanted to add 1101 to 10111 and had assigned only five binary digits for the answer we would get 100, but $13 + 23$ is not 8. The solution is to keep calm and carry on adding space.

The Americans involved in computation were, at one stage or another, working alongside each other or closely connected to other relevant people's work. Claude Shannon acted as Alan Turing's host during a visit he made to Bell Telephone Laboratories in the middle of World War II. That world war would put to use all the theorizing about logic and enable Alan Turing's concept of a programmable computing machine to become a reality. Claude Shannon did not stop at the theory of circuits either: he founded information theory as a mathematical discipline and wrote a treatise on the theory of cryptography. Computing and codes are symbiotic creatures and it was via code-breaking that the two paths of computing were about to meet.

Claude Shannon applied Boolean algebra to the practical realm of complex circuitry.

TAKE IT AWAY

Subtraction, in binary, can be done in the traditional way. Say you want to subtract 91 from 136 (or, in binary, you want to know what is 10001000 minus 1011011)?

Traditional method

Remember that each column is a multiple of 2: units, twos, fours, eights, and so on. So each column is twice the size of the one to its right, just as in decimal a column is ten times the size of the one to its right.

	Taking it in stages:	'Borrowing' effectively	Compare
10001000	10001000	means increasing the	decimal
− 1011011	−1	amount to be subtracted	calculation:
101101	?	from the higher column.	1__
	In subtracting	Showing the whole	136
	1 from 0, it is	calculation with all	− 91
	necessary to	borrowed digits in grey:	45
	'borrow' 1 from	1111111_	
	the adjacent	10001000	
	higher column.	1011011	
		101101	

Complements method

Even in decimal arithmetic, a cheat method for doing subtraction is to add complements. Finding complements in binary is very simple: invert the digits as in the Boolean operation NOT. (In the example below, the complement of 1011011 is 0100100. In other words, you change 1 to 0 and 0 to 1.) Then, just in the cheat method for decimals, you add the complement of the number to be subtracted to the larger number you are subtracting from. This is the balance, once you make the same two adjustments needed in decimal arithmetic: discard the one at the beginning of the sum and add it to the units. This splendid scheme is used in digital computer subtraction routines.

Conventional Arithmetic:	Complement of	Add complement:	Adjust ones:
10001000		10001000	
− 1011011	1011011		
101101	↓		
	0100100	+ 0100100	
		10101100	101101

Chapter 4

COMPUTING DECODED

World War II spawned a range of developments in computing, starting with the work to break the notorious Enigma cipher. Machines such as the Bombe and Colossus paved the way toward modern electronic computing machinery. The war also created a prodigious amount of computation, demanding faster, mechanized solutions. Many developments were happening in parallel, but ENIAC, an American machine that became operational in 1945, was both electronic and programmable.

The need to protect convoys and provide intelligence to troops abroad spawned rapid developments in computing technology.

The most secret problem of World War II was not, at the outset, the development of the atomic bomb. That problem and its secrecy came later. Right at the start, the problem was the Enigma machine – and it was a problem in computing.

A computing enigma

The Enigma machine was an encipherment machine developed in the inter-war years and adopted across the German armed forces for secure communications. Its supposed benefit was that the machine could be set up in

ENIGMA

The Enigma machine's job is to convert plain language into a stream of meaningless random gibberish. It is a ciphering machine, which means that each letter is converted to some other letter of the alphabet. The clever thing about Enigma is that the conversion process changes every time you press a key, because the key-stroke causes the rotors in the machine to turn.

The machine looks rather like a typewriter, but instead of printing out the typescript the output is to light up one of 26 lettered bulbs on a display panel above the keyboard. When you press a key it creates an electrical contact that eventually lights the bulb beneath the encipherment of the letter you pressed. Meanwhile, the electric current has travelled a path through the machine that ensures that the cipher-text is different from the plain language. The path goes through a plugboard, which swaps one letter for another; through three rotors, each of which is wired to divert the current along a new path; around a 'reflector' and back through the three rotors. If you press the 'A' key, it might be converted on the plugboard to K; current entering the bank of rotors along the K wire might be converted by the first rotor to M, then to E by the second and to T by the third, where it enters the reflector; emerging from the reflector at (say) W, it passes back through the three rotors, changing again every time, and then back through the plugboard it might route to the light-bulb under the letter X. And next time you press 'A', the rotors will have moved, altering the path completely, so it is likely that you will not again get the letter X.

There are 17,576 (26 × 26 × 26) configurations for the three rotors, but there was a library of five rotors to choose from, allowing for 60 ways of choosing three of the five rotors and inserting them in any order into the machine (5 × 4 × 3). Then there was the plugboard. The Germans used 10 cables, giving a huge 1.5×10^{14} further permutations (26 factorial / 10 factorial × 6 factorial × 2^{10}). Combining all these, you can choose from among 158,962,555,217,826,360,000 different ways to set up the machine. Every day.

The Enigma machine converted its messages with an almost unbreakable cipher by turning the rotors after every key stroke.

The intercepted messages provided few clues for the codebreakers at Bletchley Park.

```
1827  3225XM  C1626  W987
SEXTO


H6R  5RH DE C  1346 = 3TLE  = 2TL  224 = HUW XNG  =
DKRKI  CUZAF  MNSDC  AWXVJ  DVZNH  DMOZN  NWRJC  KKJQO
ELWIK  XDUUF  ECEGN  OUNNQ  CIIZX  FUTAF  BTNWI  GOECK
CHYUC  KTTYB  ZMDTU  WCNWH  OXOFX  ERVQV  JUCVY  PQACQ
EBHXE  NOQKF  LWRWR  LGKXZ  BPYWR  GQVYG  WJDGA  QXKVC
MQQJJ  PVSLG  WFZJZ  HHWQG  YFCQQ  RHVRR  QQIDQ  QVVIW
LJLBH  LHHDI  OFWUY  JJQGX  BWPZ
CCT 2/3  RCWGN
1852 FLC
```

150 quintillion (1.58 x 10^20) different ways and even if you had intercepted an enciphered message and possessed an Enigma machine, if you didn't know how to set up the machine for decryption it would still take until the end of the universe and beyond before you could try out all the possible settings and hit upon the right one. Only the intended recipient knew how to set up his machine for decryption and so it did not matter that the enciphered text went out on the airwaves for all to hear, or that an Enigma machine might get captured on a battlefield.

The Enigma machine takes the plain-text of a message and converts it into secret cipher-text: the process it uses to achieve this is purely mechanical and could be done by a human computer using a pencil and paper, although that would be tedious and error-prone. The same can be said when the machine is used for decryption (assuming

the recipient knows how to set up his machine).

It is now very well known that MI6, the British secret intelligence service, considered that finding a way to decipher radio-telegrams enciphered on an Enigma machine was a vital project for the Allied war effort and that a team of boffins was deployed to work on the problem at a secret location called Bletchley Park. It's no coincidence that one of the first people recruited for the attack on Enigma was Alan Turing: his appetite for challenging mathematical problems, coupled

WEATHER FORECAST

In the heyday of Enigma decryption at Bletchley Park, much depended on guesswork. The codebreakers needed to predict the content of enciphered telegrams in order to set up the Bombe to find the settings on the Enigma machine. So predictable, formulaic content of messages was extremely helpful – not only stock phrases showing due respect to the general, but things that should never have been enciphered at all because there was nothing secret in the content, such as the strategically shocking news that there was nothing to report, or the weather forecast. *Wettervorhersage* is a nice long German word, meaning sunny today to codebreakers and stormy outlook to their opponents.

with his experience (both theoretical and practical) with computing machinery, made him an ideal choice. Alan Turing was also immeasurably helped by learning on the very eve of the outbreak of war that the Polish Cipher Bureau had managed, through a feat of astonishing mathematical analysis, to reverse-engineer the wiring of the German military Enigma machine as long ago as 1932. So Bletchley did not even have to wait for a battlefield capture to begin work on a technique for solving the problem. Better still, the Poles had also developed various methods to find the settings, which the Germans were now changing on a daily basis.

Bletchley Park

In 1938, Bletchley Park was an empty mansion house, of an architectural style universally deplored, situated in large grounds just outside a railway-junction town in the south Midlands of Britain. The town itself was nondescript. Evidently it was an ideal location for acquisition by a secret government establishment; and it had hidden advantages, notably that one of the railways connected to both Oxford and Cambridge.

Oxford and Cambridge boasted professors, and the recruitment drive initiated by the secret establishment, called the Government Code and Cypher School

At the beginning of World War II, Bletchley Park was an uninhabited manor just outside a nondescript town. By the end of the war it had become the hub of the UK's codebreaking efforts, housing thousands of people.

Deciphering machines like the Bombe helped mechanize much of the work of decryption.

was the fastest way to sift through millions of pieces of data gleaned from the decrypts. Indeed, Bletchley Park should probably be seen as the first centre for processing of Big Data.

Explosive ideas (1)

Alan Turing's challenge was to find a new method for finding the settings, because the Polish technique depended on the Germans enciphering part of the setting twice over, an insecure practice that everyone was sure the Germans would change once the war heated up. (Indeed they did, at the beginning of the Battle of France in spring 1940, by which time the new mechanized attack was well into development.) Adopting the Polish idea of a machine that could automatically crank through all 17,576 possible combinations of the three coding-rotors of Enigma, Turing's own idea was to have his machine – the Bombe – test electrically whether an Enigma machine set up in a particular way could in fact yield an observed intercepted message if the original plain-text was known.

This is a slightly paradoxical way of looking at the problem: if you knew the original, why bother to waste time trying to decipher it? The whole point, surely, was that you did not know the original. But military folks like to use stereotypical expressions for convenience (and out of

sought to hire 'men of the professor type' to join its standby list in case hostilities began. Meanwhile the professors were sent on training courses to familiarize themselves with things like codes and ciphers.

When the war began, the professors arrived and rapidly overflowed the limited office space on the site. Over the first four years of the war, the landscaped gardens gave way first to wooden huts and then to brick and concrete buildings to house what eventually became an information factory staffed by around 10,000 people, very few of whom were men and even fewer of whom were professors.

Most of the people at Bletchley were engaged in some form of computing. Some were using algorithms to set up settings-finding machines like the Bombe and Colossus. Some were using Typex machines to decrypt enciphered messages. A large number were operating Hollerith punched-card machines (see pages 44–6), to which an entire building was devoted, because this

BOMBE

An unsolved mystery of World War II is how the Bombe gained its name. It's well-known that the British codebreakers wanted to pay tribute to their Polish colleagues, from whose machine (called the Bomba) some of the ideas behind the Bombe had derived. But that just restates the problem.

Various suggestions have been put forward; most of them are bunk. It's said that the original Bomba made an ominous ticking noise (partly true); it's said that the ideas came to the Poles when eating a bombe dessert in a restaurant (unverified); it is also suggested that the word *bomba* in Polish means 'splendid' (true, but no evidence to link the idea to the naming of the machine). When asked, many years after the war, one of the Polish codebreakers said it was simply because they couldn't think of a better name – which restates the problem again. The enigmatic side of World War II endures.

respect for senior military commanders to whom they are reporting). So stock-phrases like 'To the commanding general' and (yes) 'Weather forecast' could be predicted, even if this was no more than guesswork. If the guessed-at text could be enciphered in the observed way, that gave lots of letter-pairs that could be tested to try to crack the rest of the cypher.

Alan Turing's Bombe was not a 'computer' in the modern sense, but it did have some remarkable features. One of the features was that it did not work very well until modified by another of the mathematicians of Bletchley Park, Gordon Welchman, whose proposal to add cross-wiring called the 'diagonal board' hugely improved its efficiency; but setting aside the teething troubles and how the Bombe developed from prototype to factory-model,

the Bombe used a digital (not analogue) approach to testing for good or bad settings; it was programmed for each run and then fully automatic once switched on; and it was using modern, state-of-the-art electromechanical relay technology. No, you couldn't use it for arithmetic or indeed for any problem at all other than finding settings on Enigma machines, but it was certainly solving a problem in modern computation, namely how to reduce 1.58×10^{20} permutations to a more manageable number of options to be tested by hand.

The story of Bletchley Park's success is now very well known; a slightly lesser-known chapter in that story is what happened after the radio interception service started picking up a completely different type of coded message from 1940 onwards. These messages were not being sent in Morse but

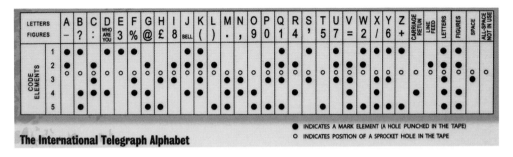

LETTERS	A	B	C	D	E	F	G	H	I	J	K	L	M	N	O	P	Q	R	S	T	U	V	W	X	Y	Z	CARRIAGE RETURN	LINE FEED	LETTERS	FIGURES	SPACE	ALL-SPACE NOT IN USE
FIGURES	-	?	:	WHO ARE YOU	3	%	@	£	8	BELL	(	)	.	,	9	0	1	4	'	5	7	=	2	/	6	+						
1	●	●		●	●	●				●	●						●		●		●		●	●	●	●			●	●		
2	●		●				●		●	●	●	●				●	●	●			●	●	●					●	●	●		
3 (sprocket)	○	○	○	○	○	○	○	○	○	○	○	○	○	○	○	○	○	○	○	○	○	○	○	○	○	○	○	○	○	○	○	○
4			●			●		●	●		●		●	●		●	●		●		●	●		●	●				●		●	
5		●	●	●		●	●			●	●		●	●	●			●				●		●			●		●	●		

The International Telegraph Alphabet

● INDICATES A MARK ELEMENT (A HOLE PUNCHED IN THE TAPE)
○ INDICATES POSITION OF A SPROCKET HOLE IN THE TAPE

From 1940, messages sent in the teleprinter code began to appear alongside Morse code.

the teleprinter code, which replaces each letter of the alphabet, the numbers 0 to 9, and various typographical symbols with a five-digit binary sequence. As with Morse code messages, the Germans were using a machine to encipher their teleprinter traffic; and as with the Enigma machine, their teleprinter cipher machines changed the cipher every time a new letter was typed. The machine was called the Lorenz Schlüsselzusatz ('cipher attachment' in English) and, unlike Enigma, the British had never seen one and the Poles had not even known of its existence, let alone been able to supply a reverse-engineered replica to them. This time the British were on their own. They didn't even know the name of the German machine, so they just called this type of message 'Fish' and the German machine 'Tunny'.

The Lorenz in-line encipherment machine automatically converted teleprinter (telex) messages into enciphered form. (By contrast, the Enigma machine merely lit up light-bulbs to inform the cipher-clerk what letter to transmit in Morse code.) Like the Enigma machine, the Lorenz worked by means of various coding-wheels, but that's more or less where the similarities stop.

The Lorenz machine had 12 wheels. Each wheel was resettable by moving pins into 'on' or 'off' positions, which would determine whether the electrical pulse passed across the wheel would be modified or not. The number of pins was deliberately chosen to be complicated: 43, 47, 51, 53,

The Lorenz machine had 12 wheels, which it used to automatically encipher teleprinter messages.

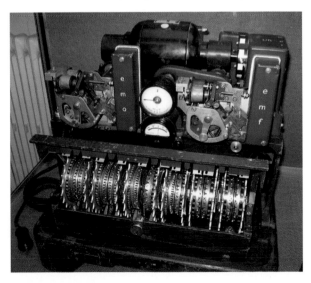

59, 37, 61, 41, 31, 29, 26 and 23 – this way the chance of all wheels realigning so as to give a repetition was extremely low. The wheels were in three groups, named after the Greek letters *chi*, *psi* and *mu* by the codebreakers at Bletchley.

The first five wheels, the *chi* wheels, modified (or, depending on the pin-settings, did not modify) the electrical footprint of the five binary characters of the teleprinted letter. So did a second bank of five wheels, the *psi* wheels. With the typing of the next letter, the five *chi* wheels always moved on, just like the right-most rotor of an Enigma machine, but whether the *psi* wheels moved on was determined by the two other wheels – the *mu* (or motor) wheels. This behaviour meant that the modifications made by the *psi* wheels might be the same for two or more successive letters – a feature that enabled the codebreakers to strip away the effect of the *psi* wheels through binary addition. In arithmetic done on a machine without the ability to carry, adding a binary number twice has no net effect.

Once again machinery came to the fore to help with the challenge of Tunny. Again an astonishing feat of analysis allowed John Tillman and Bill Tutte, two more codebreakers in the Bletchley pantheon, to understand the workings of Tunny. But just like Enigma, it was not enough to know how the machine was wired and how it worked. They needed to know how it was set up for each transmission, otherwise the intercepted messages would remain nothing more than squealings in the ether.

Wonder of the world

The method Bletchley Park would use to break into Tunny was, once again, by using a machine. This time it was the brainchild of Max Newman, Alan Turing's teacher from the days of 'On Computable Numbers' at Cambridge, and Tommy Flowers, a Post Office Telephones engineer whom Turing had introduced to Newman, in exploiting an idea of the Tunny expert Bill Tutte.

Tutte's idea was a 'statistical method' for discovering the Tunny settings. It was simple enough to describe: to count the frequency of coincidences between two streams of data, the one representing all possible combinations of the five *chi*-wheels of the encipherment machine and the other

The wheels of the Lorenz machine were separated into three groups, named chi, psi *and* mu *by the codebreakers.*

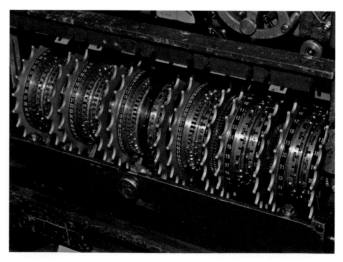

TOMMY FLOWERS AND THE COLOSSUS

Unlike the Bombe at Bletchley Park, nobody asks why the Colossus was called by that name.

Breaking the teleprinter cipher generated by the German Lorenz machine could be done by hand, but it took weeks of labour to do. A mechanized solution was needed. The first effort was a machine called 'Heath Robinson' because it was a wonderful contraption whose main feature was two long strips of punched tape which had to be run past a reader at high speed and kept in synch – which was beyond the limits of 1942 technology and had predictable results with ripped tape and conflagrations.

At the Post Office research laboratory was a young engineer called Tommy Flowers, whose speciality was electronics. Converting telephone exchanges into electronic circuits was the big mid-century project, since it would allow automated long-distance dialling – and Flowers knew exactly how to get this novel technology to work. He had been brought in to the Bletchley Park fold when there were new developments to the Bombes, but his real contribution was on the teleprinter deciphering project.

He reckoned that electronic valves could be used to replace one of the high-speed tapes completely, and he knew how to devise and build switching to enable an electronic machine to be reset, or programmed, to operate differently for different code-breaking tasks. Despite scepticism about the reliability of a machine incorporating an unprecedented number of valves (1,500 for his Mark 1 machine), Flowers persisted with his idea, delivering his first machine to Bletchley Park in late 1943. The machine was named 'Colossus', and the reduction in code-breaking time was so dramatic that an improved Mark 2 machine was promptly ordered, followed by an order for eight more. The Mark 2 was delivered in time for D-day and its results contributed significantly to the Allies' confidence that the landings in Normandy would be successful.

Flowers's work on Colossus was, like everything associated with Bletchley Park, an official secret, so after the war he returned to work on telephone exchanges. He received the MBE in 1943 but there was no other formal recognition of his achievements. Only when the story of Colossus began to emerge in the 1980s did Flowers's contribution to the story of computing begin to be understood.

representing the intercepted cipher-text. Tutte wanted to look for sequences where the correspondence was slightly better than average – about 55 per cent – as that would indicate the part of a *chi*-wheel sequence corresponding to a given set of start-positions of the *chi* wheels. The problem was that Tutte's solution would involve an immense amount of computing time if done by human computers – possibly hundreds of years per message, according to an estimate by Newman.

Newman's idea was to mechanize the comparison. The first efforts involved using photoelectric cells to count holes in two fast-moving bands of paper tape into which

---

COMPUTING WITH THE TELEPRINTER CODE

The principle on which Colossus operated was that of a strange world of circular arithmetic. If you represent the letters of the teleprinter alphabet on a punched tape, you can get something like

$$A = xx\bullet\bullet\bullet \qquad B = x\bullet\bullet xx \qquad C = \bullet xxx\bullet \qquad D = x\bullet\bullet x\bullet \qquad E = x\bullet\bullet\bullet\bullet$$

where an x means a hole has been punched and a dot means that the paper is intact. (Unfortunately modern typography makes the dots so big that they look like holes, but dots for no-mark is what the codebreakers used.)

Dots and crosses can be added as binary, circular arithmetic: indeed this is what the cipher-stream generated by the *chi*-wheels of the Lorenz machine was doing. Say that the cipher-stream threw out $\bullet x\bullet\bullet\bullet$ and the letter to be enciphered at that point was A, then the machine would add $xx\bullet\bullet\bullet$ and $\bullet x\bullet\bullet\bullet$ to get $x\bullet\bullet\bullet\bullet$ or the letter E: for $\bullet$ plus x is x, x plus x is $\bullet$ and $\bullet$ plus $\bullet$ is $\bullet$. In Boolean terms, the combination is the exclusive or, or 'XOR'.

---

both data-streams had been punched. These efforts were dogged with synchronization problems, ripped tape catching fire and an awkward combination of reliance on electrical relays and more modern electronic equipment. At this point Flowers, with his experience of electronic switching systems being pioneered in the telephone service, offered the benefit of his knowledge. He reckoned the machine could be built using the newest technology of the day: vacuum tubes, known in the UK as valves. Most people were sceptical about this, because valves blew and you'd have to spend all day working out which one had failed, like when a bulb blows on a string of Christmas-tree lights. With 1,500 valves this would hardly be practical with the failure rates common in 1943. But Tommy Flowers knew a secret: don't turn the machine off – ever. If it were left running, so that the valves weren't constantly subjected to the stresses of being warmed up and cooled down, they were far less likely to blow.

Tommy Flowers introduced the idea of vacuum tubes, or valves, to computing.

The Colossus was the machine that embraced the technology of valves and it was a far more versatile tool than the Bombe.

The valve machines, in their final production model, were named Colossus. Colossus represented a breakthrough in computing machine design: not only was the machine now based on electronic technology, but it was more versatile than the Bombe. Certainly, a Colossus was designed to solve a particular problem, namely Tunny settings, but it was programmable in a rather remarkable way. The banks of switches used to input the *chi*-wheel data-stream into Colossus were, in effect, determining the circuitry of the machine. And Newman had asked Flowers to build additional flexibility into the logical design, so that different and new problems could be run on his remarkable machine.

Tommy Flowers explained, in an interview given in 1975:

They wanted to change the logic ... and we provided them with a big panel with a lot of keys on it and by throwing the keys they – the mathematicians – could program the machine. The keys did the 'and' and 'or' functions ... and put them in series and parallel and so forth, and they were quite happy. In fact they were like a lot of schoolboys with a new toy when we first gave it to them; they thought it so wonderful they were playing with it for ages just to see what you could do with it.

The mathematician and code-breaker I.J. Good was one of Newman's team, and recalled what the 'schoolboys' in question had actually used Colossus to do:

You could do ordinary arithmetic in principle with the Colossus; it was sufficiently flexible. It took a great deal of plugging and it wasn't worthwhile ... the statistics were done just by counting, you see, not by multiplying numbers together most of the time, but ... you could in fact plug so that it would multiply.

young Konrad's vision, since they were also called upon for funding as well as to tolerate their home turning into an engineering laboratory. Konrad's first effort was not particularly successful; his second, named Z2, was just about completed when war broke out. The Z2 was followed by ever-improved machines, called Z3 and Z4, in 1941 and 1945 respectively. As the Russians approached Berlin, Zuse heaved the Z4 on to a truck and headed for Bavaria, where the Allies were in control.

Although Zuse, like his American counterparts, was using electro-magnetic relay technology for his hardware, his

Using code-breaking equipment just to see if you could do multiplication for fun was, perhaps, a bit perverse, as the war was creating quite enough multiplication sums of its own.

Germany wins the war

Despite all the strides being made with computing machinery in the United States, the experts had, unknown to all of them, been beaten by developments in Germany. There, in Berlin, an engineer called Konrad Zuse had already developed mechanical programmable calculating machinery as early as 1935. The first assembly was done in his parents' apartment: the patient senior Zuses must have been infected with

With the help of advanced computing machinery, hard work by mathematicians, and a dose of luck, the string of seemingly random letters of the intercept were converted into comprehensible German.

Germany did not lag behind the Allies in its pursuit of computers. The Z4, shown here, was the world's earliest digital computer.

approach to problem-solving was novel. He devised a programming language called *Plankalkül* (or 'plan-based system'), which envisioned a two-dimensional map, with different operations allocated to different places. Zuse soon realized that there was no need for a physical map, since the important thing was to get the machine to go to the locations in the right order: the sequence of the operations was the thing that mattered. The 'plan' was a series of go-to instructions, specific to the 'calculation', and could be changed depending on what he wanted the machine to do. Zuse's machines were all built around this fundamental idea of a sequenced program. The underlying conceptual work had been done in 1934, even before Alan Turing had begun his work 'On Computable Numbers' over in Cambridge. Zuse's approach had separate units for arithmetical operations, control and memory, with punched paper tape as program input. All these developments

Konrad Zuse began assembling computers in his parents' apartment. His innovations anticipated the post-war developments of the industry in Britain and the United States.

anticipated the post-war design and structure of Anglo-American computer design.

Explosive ideas (2)

The constant invention and reinvention of weapons was generating a prodigious amount of computing to be done. There were various solutions. First, to increase the number of human computers, even by radical means.

Another idea was to rely on more machinery. Expensive and delicate analogue machines such as differential analysers were all very well in their specialist place but, to deal with the sheer volume of computing requirements, they were not the way forward. Electricity had its champions, in particular at the Bell Telephone Laboratories. Bell Labs developed anti-aircraft gunnery computing machines that used electrical circuitry where traditional analogue computing machines would have used moving mechanical parts. Circuitry could replace the precision-engineered components and could be mass-produced quickly, cheaply and accurately. Another particular advantage of electrical systems is that the input into the computation could be fed directly from other devices, such as radar systems. Some of the analogue devices using electricity were superb: the M-9

While they waited for new machines to be developed, the US government greatly increased the number of human computers.

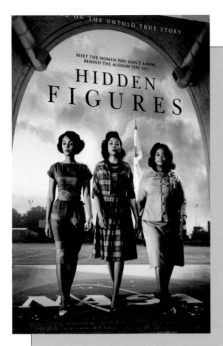

In 1943, non-white computers began to be employed at Langley, Virginia. Many continued into highly successful and prestigious roles at NASA.

'COLORED COMPUTERS'

In 1941, by Executive Order No. 8802, President Franklin D. Roosevelt abolished racial segregation in the United States defence industry. By 1943, desegregation had come to be seen as a solution to the shortage of human computers, and at the end of that year the first non-white female computers began work in Langley, VA, operating mechanical desk calculators to carry out complex mathematical operations. It wasn't easy for them. For months, they were expected to eat their lunch at a special table that was labelled 'Colored Computers'. They also had a segregated bathroom. Desegregation, it seemed, only went so far. Theirs is an uplifting story, because they got rid of the label from the lunch-room and, crumb by crumb, they dismantled the other prejudices of their co-workers. Those women would go on to hold prestigious roles in programming modern computing machinery in the post-war period and are now recognized for their front-line role in another war, the one for equality.

anti-aircraft-missile director, for example, shot down 89 out of 91 V1 flying bombs launched at London in August 1944.

Shooting down aircraft, or V1 flying bombs, generates vast volumes of computation. Each new gun that comes into use requires its own firing tables, or some sort of aiming mechanism that has in-built computation. But the development of entirely new weapons lifted the computation needs of the United States to an entirely new level: the complexity of the equations that had to be solved in order to develop the hydrogen bomb was unprecedented.

Fortunately for the future of nuclear calculations, a project had been given the go-ahead in 1943: the building of a vast new computing machine to calculate trajectories, which depend not just on weight, muzzle velocity, wind speed and air density, but more problematically on the amount of drag experienced by the missile, which is a function of the square of the missile's speed, which itself is reduced by the drag. Like the Colossus in Britain (although nobody appears to have known about the parallel developments), the American project would exploit the speed of electronic valves to carry out calculations. The new machine would take two years to build and would have 17,468 valves, 70,000 resistors, 10,000 capacitors, 7,200 crystal diodes, 20 accumulators, a high-speed multiplier, three function table units, a divider and a square-rooter. It would

TALE OF TWO PHONE COMPANIES

It was the best of times for phone companies' research departments, even if it was the worst of times for those fighting the actual war. Bell Telephone Laboratories in Manhattan had a number of mould-breaking projects afoot. These included building cryptological Bombes for the US Army, creating a speech-encipherment system for secure phone-calls and developing electrical computation machinery. It is perhaps no coincidence that the most imaginative engineers dealing with highly complex electrical and electronic technology worked for the phone company – the same was true in Britain. Tommy Flowers, the chief engineer of the Colossus, was an engineer of the Post Office Research Station in London.

Bell Telephone Laboratories in Manhattan was the site of many important developments in computing.

occupy a room the size of a basketball court. Its inelegant name was Electronic Numerical Integrator and Calculator (ENIAC). The project was plagued with the familiar problem of valves blowing. Independently, the Americans solved the problem in the way that Tommy Flowers had for Colossus: you just left the thing switched on.

John von Neumann, who had needed to model the behaviour of a shock wave in order to ensure that a piece of plutonium imploded properly, had his bomb calculations

Dealing with the threat of V1 rockets required a more efficient way of solving mathematical problems.

ENIAC was America's room-sized response to the threats of World War II.

revolution in computers, as it firmly established electronics as being central to computing machinery. Like the atomic bomb, it made all other weapons of assault on computing look like historical artefacts. The contrast with 1937, although a great year of innovation, was extreme: in 1945, the future of computing looked very different.

performed by human computers aided by punched cards. Von Neumann was delighted when he learned about ENIAC, and when ENIAC was ready to run its first calculations at around Christmas 1945 it was quickly deployed for atomic computations rather than artillery trajectories.

ENIAC has been described as a hardware

The technological developments that had allowed the invention of Colossus, ENIAC and the Z2 pointed the way forward: multi-purpose electronic computing machines could take over the role of differential analysers, electro-mechanical calculators and other delicate, expensive equipment used as aids for computation.

ENIAC v. COLOSSUS

ENIAC was commissioned in May 1943, about the same time as Bletchley Park began work on machine solutions to the Tunny problem. ENIAC was finished in 1945 and it ran its first program after the war had ended. Colossus was up and running in time for D-day in June 1944. Colossus remained a secret for a very long time, in view of the specialist and secret nature of the problems it was being asked to solve, with reasonably full details not being released until 50 years after the war had ended. By contrast, ENIAC's purpose was not a secret, even if the purpose of the calculations it was asked to do were. So the world learned about ENIAC first and here a controversy was born. Who got there first, the Americans (as everyone believed for many years) or the British?

The answer probably doesn't matter, but here it is. The British machine was operational first, but it was very narrowly purposed and – as I.J. Good explained – it was all but useless for general computation. ENIAC, by contrast, was an all-purpose machine, even if it got over the line a year later. Neither of them was a stored-program computer in the modern sense, so the actual answer is 'neither', even though both machines occupy places of honour in the history of computing machinery.

Chapter 5

MARCH OF THE MACHINES

Electronic computation started with
the building of an electrical circuit to
carry out simple arithmetical operations.
Larger, electro-mechanical machines
developed the ideas and could be reset,
or programmed, to do different tasks.
In the post-war period the concept of
a program stored within the machine's
memory became a reality, with
computing machine projects in both
America and Britain. Innovative solutions
were found to challenges with the
technology, particularly memory.

Large, room-sized electro-mechanical computers
dominated the post-war industry. Here, a man
prepares a Univac computer to predict a winning
horse in 1959.

ENIAC did not suddenly emerge from nowhere. In the United States, immediately before the war, there had been a significant amount of invention and creativity in the field of automated calculation.

The year 1937 had been a prodigious one for the development of computing machines. Among the remarkable team of innovators at Bell Labs was an engineer called George R. Stibitz, who had been involved in the computing system used in the M-9 anti-aircraft missile director and who had another idea that would radically reshape the way that electricity could be used for computing problems. Stibitz observed that the two states of a telephone relay were analogous to the on-off nature of binary arithmetic. In 1937 he started to play with the idea, starting with a home-made device that could carry out addition.

George R. Stibitz, an engineer at Bell Labs, made his most important discoveries at home. His ideas shaped how computer circuits were to be designed going forward.

The 'Model K' computer was named after the kitchen table on which it was built.

K IS FOR KITCHEN

George Stibitz's insight came at home. Although he used two spare relays from the rubbish-bin at Bell Labs, everything else was built on the kitchen table. He used bits of a tobacco tin, some batteries, torch bulbs and a scrap of old plywood. From all this he constructed his adder circuit, showed it to his boss at Bell Labs and from there the idea of circuitry design specifically for computational problems began. Dorothea Stibitz, George's wife, named the original device the 'Model K', after the kitchen table where it all began.

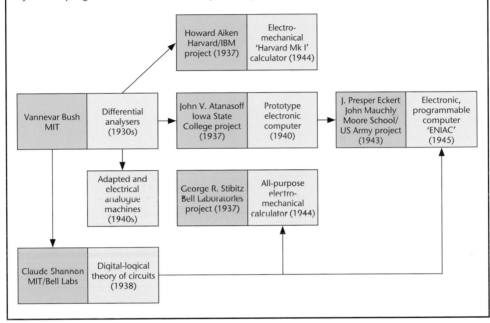

DOUBLE DIGIT DISCOVERIES

In the 1930s, several American inventors simultaneously began projects to turn computing machinery digital. These proceeded in parallel, with their own specificities, until superseded by stored-program electronic machinery in the post-war period.

Howard Aiken Harvard/IBM project (1937)	Electro-mechanical 'Harvard Mk I' calculator (1944)

Vannevar Bush MIT	Differential analysers (1930s)

John V. Atanasoff Iowa State College project (1937)	Prototype electronic computer (1940)

J. Presper Eckert John Mauchly Moore School/ US Army project (1943)	Electronic, programmable computer 'ENIAC' (1945)

Adapted and electrical analogue machines (1940s)	

George R. Stibitz Bell Laboratories project (1937)	All-purpose electro-mechanical calculator (1944)

Claude Shannon MIT/Bell Labs	Digital-logical theory of circuits (1938)

Circuitous approach

Stibitz's idea led rapidly to the design of circuits that could carry out arithmetical operations. Electrical machines, coupled with switching technology, could be made to do computing. Contemporaneously with Stibitz's work, there were two other developments in the US that were taking calculating machinery into another dimension. Each of the groups thinking about machines was becoming dissatisfied with the time required to set up a differential analyser to run a problem – it could be as much as two days – and the other challenges of using analogue machines. While some groups felt that adding punched-tape,

electrical or even electronic components to an analogue machine could improve its performance, other teams were going digital.

One of the initiatives was at Harvard. In 1937, a graduate student called Howard Aiken had come up with ideas about digital computing, wanting to break away from the constraints of punched cards and adding machines. Influenced by a demonstration model of Babbage's Difference Engine No.1, he wanted to build an automatic calculator to take out the tedium and delays associated with roomfuls of human computers. Aiken would have preferred cutting-edge electronic technology, but budgets were tight and effective delivery of the project could be assured by partnering with IBM. Aiken's plan was to automate computation, so that arithmetical operations would take place in a controlled sequence. The machine was finished in mid-1944 and initially called the IBM Automatic Sequence Controlled Calculator. A bank of knobs was used to input data in decimal numbers. There were 72 'accumulators', consisting of electromagnetic counter-wheels; if a number was directed to an accumulator, it added it to whatever number was already there. The accumulators could also do subtraction, using the method of complements as in a mechanical adding-machine. There were

THE NAVY BUG

Join the Navy, see the world. It's surprising how often that turns out not to be true: ask the women who served in the WRNS (UK) or as WAVES (US) and worked on decryption machines in World War II. Grace Hopper was another woman who, on being commissioned into the US Navy in 1944, found herself assigned to the Harvard University computation project – perhaps not such a surprise when you know that she had a top-class degree in mathematics and physics from Vassar College, an MA, a PhD and the CV of a mathematics professor of ten years' seniority.

On arrival, Lieutenant Hopper was greeted thus: 'Where the hell have you been?' Her superior officer was Lieutenant Commander Howard Aiken, US Naval Reserve, and his orders were for her to compute the coefficients of the arc-tan series, on his machine, by Tuesday. 'I had never met a digit and I wanted nothing to do with digits,' she said later, but in the Navy, orders are orders. Grace Hopper not only became an expert programmer and the author of the Harvard Mark I's manual of operations but went on to devote her career to programming. She was a tireless champion of women in technology and had been promoted to Rear-Admiral by the time she retired from the US Navy.

Among her achievements was the first documented debugging of a program. In 1945, Hopper was investigating the failure in the operation of the Mark II machine then in use at Harvard. In the logbook, she wrote 'First actual case of bug being found.' A moth had got caught in the machine and disabled a relay. Although she denied this was the first such usage of the term, it's good to know that in the Navy, bugs are bugs.

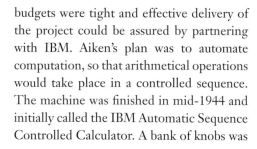

The original 'bug' in computing was found by Grace Hopper and diligently recorded in her notes.

For the Harvard Mark I computer, a roll of punched tape was used to input instructions.

it was small because it depended on valves (vacuum tubes) for its logical processing. The memory was made up of a drum-shaped device with the storage elements provided by small capacitors studded around the curved surface. It was more or less a proof-of-concept device and its input-output mechanism needed refinement; but it worked all right to solve simultaneous equations with a large number of variables.

For reasons outside Atanasoff's control, the computing machine he had built went nowhere. It was not until the appearance of John Mauchly, whose drive and energy lay behind the ENIAC project, that any progress was made. Mauchly saw in Atanasoff's machine the potential for binary arithmetic in conjunction with electronic technology. However, in Mauchly's visit to Ames lay the roots of many years of embittered litigation over originality.

also units for multiplying and dividing and counting and most importantly for controlling the sequence of operation. Instructions were input via punched tape and results output on to IBM punched cards. Not surprisingly, it was vast: 2.5m (8ft) high, 16m (51ft) long, 4,500kg (10,000lbs) in weight, with 850km of wire and 3,500 relays. And it was robust, computing until 1959.

The other major American initiative of this era was taking place in Ames, Iowa, where John V. Atanasoff was thinking about computing machinery in a different way. Unlike so many of the early computers, Atanasoff's computing machine was compact. It was about the size of a large desk and

John V. Atanasoff, from Iowa State University, was one of the first engineers to design a compact computer.

The Atanasoff-Berry Computer was a marvel of its time. Only the size of a large desk, it could solve multiple problems, but unlike its later competitors, it was limited in scope.

Battle of writs

It's all about cash. Imagine you had invented the electronic digital computer back in 1945 and had patented it… well, you could be very rich indeed. So it is perhaps not surprising that a good deal of time and a very great deal of money was spent during the 20th century in deciding who exactly had invented the computer and who had the rights to the royalties.

Various patents relating to the ENIAC machine developed at the end of World War II were owned by the Sperry Rand Corporation. IBM, which wanted to develop its own computing machines, was sued by Sperry Rand; IBM counter-sued; the case was settled, but IBM agreed to pay Sperry Rand 1 per cent of the cost of IBM equipment covered by the ENIAC patents. There was litigation between Bell Laboratories and Sperry Rand – resulting in more cash for Sperry Rand. When the ENIAC patents were issued in favour of

---

DRIVEN TO DRINK

In January 1937, John V. Atanasoff was stuck. He wanted to design a computing machine, but the ideas wouldn't come together. So, to clear his head, he went for a drive on the empty winter roads. His drive lasted for about 200 miles (320km) all the way to and beyond the state line marking the border between Iowa and Illinois. Unlike Iowa, Illinois allowed travellers to buy a drink, which is what Atanasoff did, though that was not the purpose of his drive. Somehow, the drink and the drive pulled the pieces together:

- Electricity and electronics, not mechanical moving parts, for the logical backbone of the machine; in particular, 'carries' would not be done by a gear-teeth/ratchet mechanism but using vacuum tubes.
- Binary, not decimal, numbers and computing by digital logic, not measurement as in an analogue device.
- Condensers (capacitors) for electrical storage of data (the computer's memory) and automatic 'refreshment of memory' to regenerate waning charge in the condensers.

The roadside bar had paper napkins, so Atanasoff was able to write down some of these thoughts. And then he had to drive all the way back to Ames, Iowa.

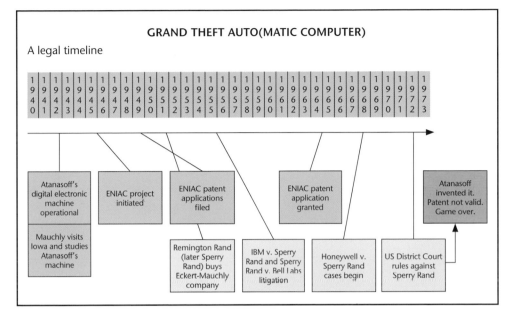

GRAND THEFT AUTO(MATIC COMPUTER)

A legal timeline

| 1940 | 1941 | 1942 | 1943 | 1944 | 1945 | 1946 | 1947 | 1948 | 1949 | 1950 | 1951 | 1952 | 1953 | 1954 | 1955 | 1956 | 1957 | 1958 | 1959 | 1960 | 1961 | 1962 | 1963 | 1964 | 1965 | 1966 | 1967 | 1968 | 1969 | 1970 | 1971 | 1972 | 1973 |

Atanasoff's digital electronic machine operational

ENIAC project initiated

ENIAC patent applications filed

ENIAC patent application granted

Atanasoff invented it. Patent not valid. Game over.

Mauchly visits Iowa and studies Atanasoff's machine

Remington Rand (later Sperry Rand) buys Eckert-Mauchly company

IBM v. Sperry Rand and Sperry Rand v. Bell Labs litigation

Honeywell v. Sperry Rand cases begin

US District Court rules against Sperry Rand

Sperry Rand in 1964, Sperry Rand checked out the list of possible patent infringers – companies like GE, Honeywell and NCR – to see who else they could challenge. The bounty was estimated at 10 million dollars – the company was going to be very rich and its shareholders very happy.

Except for the diligence of Honeywell, who sued Sperry Rand, claiming that the ENIAC patents were wrongly awarded. In fact, as the judge held in 1971, the patented parts of the ENIAC computer – things like electronic digital technology and automatically refreshing memory – had not been invented by John Mauchly or

The Sperry Rand Corporation, producer of the Univac computer, fought hard to retain the ENIAC patents.

John von Neumann (1903-57) was a true mathematical genius. A chance meeting at a railway station brought him into the computing world.

Sperry Rand, but by John V. Atanasoff, from whom Mauchly had derived them. So the ENIAC patents were invalid for want of invention. This may be why Sperry Rand is no longer a household name in the manufacture of computers, and why Atanasoff's should be.

John von Neumann

In some ways, the portrait of John von Neumann (1903–57) is like a photographic negative when compared to that of Alan Turing: a similar shape, except that the colours are reversed. Born into a moderately wealthy family in Hungary, he emigrated to America and died at the age of 54. He worked on an astonishing array of problems and is regarded as one of the 20th century's mathematical geniuses. Similarly, Alan Turing: born into a moderately unwealthy family whose roots were in India, but living in Britain and dying aged not quite 42. The breadth and quality of his studies rank him among the

20th century's geniuses too. But there the similarities stop.

John von Neumann loved life and lived it to the full. He married twice, enjoyed the company of women, drove fast cars too fast, loved food, drink, bad jokes and good company and could switch on the charm and deploy irresistible persuasion when it was called for. He spoke and wrote clearly and engagingly, even if he had the peculiar habit, when writing on a blackboard, of confining himself to a small area about 50cm (20in) across. His intellect was towering: he started with a paper on polynomials, published when he was only 17; then a book on quantum mechanics in 1932 and on to set theory, game theory, computer design, economics, fluid mechanics and very very big explosions. He could also do exceedingly complex pieces of arithmetic and analysis in his head, a talent that he sometimes had to hide from more pedestrian colleagues.

In 1943, John von Neumann visited the United Kingdom, as an expert in the behaviour of explosions and shock waves. When he returned to the United States, a chance meeting on a railway station in Maryland gave von Neumann the news that an electronic computing machine capable of 333 multiplications per second was being built only 120km (75 miles) away in Philadelphia. That machine was ENIAC and von Neumann's interest ensured he got an early opportunity to visit. ENIAC's chief engineer, J. Presper Eckert, had not met von Neumann, but knew of his reputation:

Eckert said he could tell whether von Neumann really was such a genius, if von Neumann's first question was about the logical structure of the machine. Needless to say, von Neumann passed the test.

ENIAC was bigger – much bigger – than Atanasoff's electronic computing machine. ENIAC had a clock/counter mechanism that was the secret to its speed and its programmability gave it an unprecedented

ENIAC IS NOT A FRIDGE

The iconography of computer advertising is a subject worthy of its own book. Dashing young men wearing 1970s haircuts. Awful line-drawings of uninteresting boxes that look like fridges. Coloured photos of monitors with lists of dull technical data. Maybe all of these were better than the advertisements for mainframes that filled the colour supplements of the 1960s, in which female models were decorously draped over machines as if they were sports cars. Evidently the advertising agents believed that selection and purchasing of computers was done by men with something to prove about their manhood. 'Refrigerator Ladies' is a pejorative term for the models appearing in such photos.

Kathy Kleinman is a researcher who stumbled upon a photo of ENIAC showing a handful of women holding parts of the machine. Wondering who they were and what their roles were, she was told they were Refrigerator Ladies. Nothing could have been further from the truth.

These women were the programmers. There were six in all, originally hired as computers by the US Army, but in 1945 they were put on to ENIAC. They were Jean Jennings, Marlyn Wescoff, Ruth Lichterman, Betty Snyder, Frances Bilas and Kay McNulty, with a variety of backgrounds: Jewish, Catholic, Protestant and Quaker. They were not intellectual slouches: they had to understand the mathematics in order to operate the machine. They were given blueprints and wiring diagrams and told to work out for themselves how to program it. And then they were told that the problem they had to put on the machine was

for some folks from Los Alamos – a Monte-Carlo simulation of neutron decay during nuclear fission – 'and that was when all the fun began'.

The four women holding parts of ENIAC in this photograph were programmers, not models.

versatility. Programming ENIAC involved a Bombe-like entanglement of cables and cross-pluggings, entering numerical inputs via dials. Each problem took not hours but days to set up on the machine. Due to its complexities, working on ENIAC was a specialist occupation, putting its people in the vanguard of technology.

It wasn't just the frustration of programming that showed that ENIAC's design was not the way forward. Other limitations of ENIAC were its architecture and limited memory capacity. It was, to say the least, going to be difficult to deploy ENIAC to work on the complex problems that John von Neumann carried around in his head.

The computer is born

Von Neumann, who had worked with Alan Turing in the 1930s and even offered him a job at his Institute for Advanced Study in Princeton, New Jersey, had read and (being von Neumann) understood Turing's paper 'On Computable Numbers' and could see that the solution was the stored program. All that plugging and so forth could and should be encoded and fed into a computing machine, just like a data input. It was time to think of a new design for a computing machine. During the spring and early summer of 1945, discussions between von Neumann and the ENIAC team began to mature. A new concept of computing

machine was proposed – an Electronic Discrete Variable Calculator. To modern eyes, the names given to early computing machines may seem rather clumsy, but the clumsy name says a great deal:

- ENIAC – Electronic Numerical Integrator and Computer: the innovation in this machine was its ability to do electronically and numerically what had been done by human computers using differential analysers (which, despite their name, are machines that perform *integral* calculus and operate by measuring rotations that approximate to the quantity being calculated, rather than by processing of numbers).
- EDVAC – Electronic Discrete Variable Calculator: this machine was also going to be fully electronic – and to emphasize its

A man demonstrates the operation of the EDVAC.

ODE

On 18 February 1946, an 'Ode to the ENIAC' appeared in the *Chicago Daily Tribune*:

> Well, how d'you like this new
> knick-knack,
> The Wonderful Answering ENIAC?
> With thirty tons of mechanical brains,
> It multiplies, adds, divides, explains.

Seventy years on, it's difficult to imagine a computer inspiring someone to write poetry. Or maybe that wasn't poetry.

digital, not analogue, nature, it would handle 'discrete' (non-continuous) variables. And it would not behave at all like a human computer sitting in front of an adding machine, it would do the whole calculation from start to finish, working out for itself what needed to be done next.

At the conclusion of the discussions John von Neumann went away to write up what they planned. His typescript, entitled 'First Draft of a Report on the EDVAC', ran to 100 pages. Only a handful of copies were produced, since there is a natural limit to the number of carbon-copies that can be turned out on a 1940s typewriter. The copies were liberally shared, which was

John Mauchly and J. Presper Eckert, the designers of America's first commercial computer, look over data derived from the Univac.

consistent with von Neumann's opinion that intellectual achievements should be published. And thereby John von Neumann nearly started another war.

For the only name on the title page was von Neumann's, despite it being a collaborative effort; maybe this was just a secretary's assumption, taking von Neumann's dictation, that it was his sole work. In any case it was only a first draft. But von Neumann garnered all the credit for the content of the Report, which set out breakthrough ideas on how a stored-program computer should be organized. On the other hand, the mindset of Mauchly and Eckert was focused in an entrepreneurial way on protection of intellectual property, royalties, fees, licensing and money. Bandying trade secrets around in public was no way to protect them. It may have been insulting to leave their names off the document, but it was financially damaging to distribute it. They filed a patent claim in 1947, but the wide disclosures made in 1945 rendered it invalid. Although von Neumann died in 1957, the war over patents would carry on

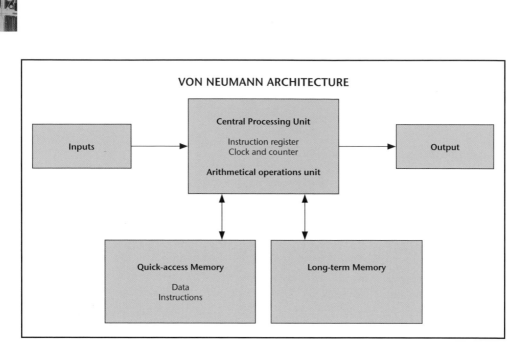

VON NEUMANN ARCHITECTURE

for many years, always with John Mauchly at its centre.

Because the 'First Draft of a Report on the EDVAC' has John von Neumann's name on its cover, its description of the organization of an electronic stored-program computer has become known as the 'von Neumann architecture'. The computer is built up out of blocks with different functions. The critical question is how they fit together and how instructions, data and results travel systematically from one point to another. With a mechanical system, or an electro-mechanical system, this was reasonably straightforward; with electronics, most of what happens is taking place at the speed of light, but then there are delays in waiting for data to emerge from memory, creating a risk that things might happen in the wrong order. The von Neumann architecture thus has a clock to keep things in synchronicity and regulation of data-flow so that instructions being fetched from short-term memory don't get confounded with data that are being processed.

The elephant problem

One fortunate recipient of the wanton distribution of the *First Draft* was Alan Turing. By mid-1945, the British establishment had worked out for itself that World War II technology should be redeployed in computing: it wasn't just the highly secret Colossus that had showed that electronics could speed up computing processes. While various universities were going to try out some research into computing machinery, the state itself would also have a go. Recognizing the growing need for 'general mathematical computation', the National Physical Laboratory, a subsidiary element of the Department of Scientific and Industrial Research, established a 'Mathematics Division' in late 1944. Alan Turing read the *First Draft* in June 1945, joined the NPL in October 1945 and had written a paper setting out a proposal for a British answer to EDVAC before Christmas. Alan Turing's computing machine was – with due respect to Charles Babbage – going to be called the Automatic Computing Engine, or ACE. It was, very possibly, going to be one of a kind.

> 'Dr Turing explained to the Executive Committee of the NPL that if a high overall computing speed was to be obtained it was necessary to do all operations automatically. It was not sufficient to do the arithmetical operations at electronic speeds: provision must also be made for the transfer of data (numbers and so on) from place to place. This led to two further requirements – 'storage' or 'memory' for the numbers not immediately in use, and means for instructing the machine to do the right operations in the right order.'

The Committee approved it, but there it was: one of the main technical challenges of computing machines in the late 1940s was how a machine could be made to remember things. Elephants might never forget, but computing machinery might be less reliable. Mechanical devices like Babbage's drums could just be left in a particular position, which would 'remember' just by staying put. Electronic devices do not behave that way. Other technologies were available for storing data for processing by a computer, but in 1945 most of them were physical in form: you could punch holes in tape, for example, and run the tape through a reader to find the data the program needed, like as had been done with Colossus. Punched cards continued to be an integral part of data-entry for a while, but for random-access memory they were almost useless.

Another physical solution was to use a 'delay line'. The principle of the delay line was to exploit the fact that a pulse of sound travels quite slowly up a tube filled with mercury; the sound wave can be picked up by a sensor at the end of its journey and pinged back down the tube, so storing the piece of data indefinitely. The problem with delay lines is implied in their name – they are slow. You would need to adjust your program so that the piece of data – the sound wave – would be available to be read by the sensor at just the right time, otherwise

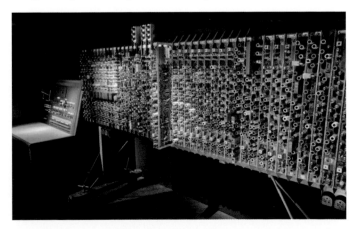

The Pilot Automatic Computing Engine, or ACE, was designed by Alan Turing and built at the National Physical Laboratory in the UK. Unlike other computers of the time, it did not include hardware for arithmetical computations, but instead relied on software.

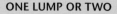

ONE LUMP OR TWO

On Tuesday 19 March 1946, the Executive Committee of Britain's National Physical Laboratory endorsed the construction of 'an automatic computing engine', as proposed by Alan Turing. With a clock speed of 1 MHz, 6000 valves, four magnetic drums, mercury delay lines for 768 numbers and punched-card input and output devices, the ACE was going to be a huge lump of a computer. When built, it filled a double-height room the size of an auditorium.

Sir Charles Darwin, the NPL's Director, had written: 'In view of its rapidity of action, and of the ease with which it can be switched over from one type of problem to another it is very possible that the one machine would suffice to solve all the problems that are demanded of it from the whole country.'

One of the committee members wanted to know whether it would be possible to have a second machine for armaments research. As the tea was poured, the committee debated the cost of duplicating the ACE. Sir Charles would need a very large supply of tea to swallow a second lump.

the program would have to sit and wait for the information. Electronic programs operating at the speed of electricity would rumble along in the slow lane while they waited for data retrieval happening at the speed of sound in mercury.

An alternative to these physical storage devices (again like Colossus) was to store some of the information electronically in valves, but valves were expensive. A third possibility was to exploit the fade characteristics of a luminous dot on a Cathode Ray Tube (CRT – a kind of small monochrome TV monitor). The CRT method was faster than delay lines and TV-screen technology had another advantage, which was that its two-dimensional surface allowed for an array of dots and blank spaces facilitating random access, rather than having to wait for the exact moment in time when the exact piece of data plops out of a one-dimensional delay line.

A tube filled with mercury was one solution to the memory problem. But delay lines relied on sound waves, which were slow, and the technology would never catch on because of this.

Cathode Ray Tubes used the fading characteristics of luminous dots to store information, and, crucially, allowed random access.

Delays on the line

Although the NPL and its executives may have considered a single computer to be sufficient for all imaginable computing needs and could back its development with the power and funding of the state, their project moved with the speed of a frozen mammoth, rather than a charging elephant. It took limitless internal wrangling to get even to the point where an intermediate-size assembly called 'Pilot ACE' was able to run a program, in May 1950. The full-size machine did not get finished until 1958, by which time Alan Turing had been dead for four years. Other pioneers were ready to march into the gap left by static bureaucracy.

The great rival to the ACE, also using delay-line memory, was Maurice Wilkes's EDSAC (Electronic Delay Storage Automatic Calculator) project at Cambridge University. Like the NPL, Wilkes's objective was a computing bureau that could accept computational problems presented by other

---

EVOLUTION: ELEPHANT TO RAM

An elephant never forgets. A common enough saying, but unlike some other proverbs it is probably a modified version of an older saying that a camel never forgets an injury – modified because natural historians have discovered, relatively recently, the prodigious memory abilities of pachyderms.

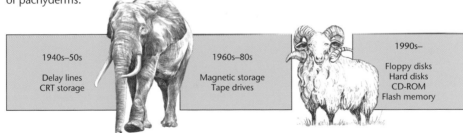

1940s–50s

Delay lines
CRT storage

1960s–80s

Magnetic storage
Tape drives

1990s–

Floppy disks
Hard disks
CD-ROM
Flash memory

Unfortunately elephants and camels don't often wish to be wired up to a mainframe. Finding a reliable, cheap way for a machine to store data was one of the biggest engineering challenges for the designers of early computers. The first solutions impeded programs, as waiting to get the data out of memory could delay the next operation.

CRT and magnetic storage solved the delay problem, and magnetic tape was cheap. But reels of tape do not allow for speedy random access, unlike a disk-based memory system. RAM was the next requirement. Solid-state technology based on silicon provides compact, random-access storage around which modern portable devices are built.

---

parts of the University. His project was more versatile, in that he was ready to adopt new hardware as it became available, simpler in the way EDSAC was programmed and free from the bureaucracy that beset the ACE. Building and operating EDSAC had challenges typical for the times:

- The building chosen for the construction of EDSAC had previously housed the Anatomy School. 'In the summer ... the formalin (used to preserve cadavers) that had impregnated the floorboards over the years was vaporized by the heat. The smell of formalin vapour is very penetrating!' (John Bennett, research student, 1947–50)
- 'EDSAC 1 was a rather recalcitrant sort of computer. Sometimes the valves rose up in their seats and got loose, overheating. So you just gave it a hearty kick, and sometimes that got it going again. We also had a lot of trouble with things setting on fire because the engineers kept joining bits on without calculating whether there were any power supplies available to feed these things.' (Lucy Slater, user of EDSAC to calculate solutions to Schrödinger's equation, 1951)

Leftovers and radioactivity

In Manchester, another project was under way. Max Newman, who had taught Alan Turing at Cambridge and then run the Colossus project at Bletchley, had been appointed Fielden Professor of Mathematics and he too was trying to build a computing machine. He begged some left-overs from Bletchley Park, to start off his project:

Manchester's project had the benefit of the emerging CRT memory technology, but it too had its teething troubles. The computer was being built in Ernest Rutherford's old building

> *To:- D.D.(A). From:- M.H.A. Newman. Date:- 8th August, 1945. After going round the equipment with me, Professor Jackson [of Manchester University] thinks the proper request for us to make is for the material of two complete Colossi; and in addition a few thousand miscellaneous resistances and condensers off other machines.*
>
> *From:– [Admin.]*
> *Date:- 8th November, 1945.*
> *D.D.(A) asked me to get in touch with you to arrange ... for the transportation of some equipment for Professor Newman ... The equipment consists of three large items ... Total weight 7 tons.*

where he had split the atom in 1917. In this faintly radioactive environment was the Royal Society Computing Machine Laboratory, described by F.C. Williams in his article 'Early Computers at Manchester University':

> *A fine sounding phrase, but what was the reality? It was one room in a Victorian building whose architectural features are best described as 'late lavatorial'. The walls were of brown glazed brick and the door was labelled 'Magnetism Room'.*

Relations were cordial to begin with, with knowhow being shared across the different projects. But rivalry and differences of opinion on coding and machine architecture occasionally caused friction. One source of annoyance for Sir Charles Darwin of the NPL was when Max Newman 'stole away' Alan Turing, who was bored with the lack of

Maurice Wilkes had a strained relationship with Alan Turing.

STAR WARS

Alan Turing and Sir Maurice Wilkes were among the most inventive and respected of the post-war computer pioneers. They were both educated at Cambridge and both scored 'starred firsts' in mathematics in their final exams in 1932. Despite these common points of interest, they couldn't get on. What was the problem?

It may have been that their social backgrounds were rather different: Alan Turing's father had been a senior officer in the upper-crust Indian Civil Service, whereas Maurice Wilkes's father had worked as an administrator for the Earl of Dudley. Or it might be that Turing's ideas were visionary, whereas Wilkes thought of computing as a utility for his University's researchers' number-crunching needs. Maybe it was because Alan Turing believed computer programs should fit the limitations of the hardware. 'I have read Wilkes' proposals... The "code" which he suggests is however very contrary to the line of development here, and much more in the American tradition of solving one's difficulties by means of much equipment rather than by thought.'

Oh dear. In public, professorial politeness was always observed and in his memoirs Wilkes made complimentary remarks about Turing. But it was a good idea to sit them at different tables during a conference dinner.

practical progress in Darwin's organization, to join him in Manchester as deputy director of his laboratory. Another was Alan Turing's inability to see eye-to-eye with Maurice Wilkes.

To move on from hardware problems to the capabilities of the new technology was heady, perhaps fanciful, stuff for 1947 and not designed to appeal to the utilitarian mindset of the NPL or the University Computing Service at Cambridge. Another stew was cooking and Alan Turing wanted to be one of the chefs (see Chapter 9). Computing would soon escape from the academic world and become an indispensable aid to the business community.

Alan Turing's move was symptomatic of a shift in the direction of computing. To quote Sir Charles Darwin, writing in 1947:

Dr A. Turing ... is the mathematician who has designed the theoretical part of our big computing engine. This has now got to the stage of ironmongery, and so for the time the chief work on it is passing into other hands... He wants to extend his work ... I can best describe it by saying that hitherto the machine has been planned for work equivalent to that of the lower parts of the brain, and he wants to see how much a machine can do for the higher ones; for example, could a machine be made that could learn by experience?

Chapter 6

THINKING INSIDE THE BOX

Computing machines were not just for
mathematicians. Business computing,
with its different needs, began to take
off in the 1950s. Software developed
from machine-specific coding to a more
general arrangement using computing
languages. Software was unbundled from
hardware and became an industry in its
own right, and in due course the idea
of making computing machines easier
for customers to use – to improve the
interface – was recognized.

*From the 1950s, computers made their way from
the universities into businesses. The ARC computer
at NASA was typical of the bulky nature of the
machines during this era.*

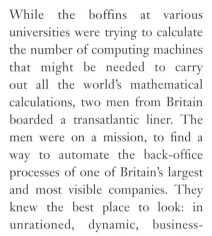

While the boffins at various universities were trying to calculate the number of computing machines that might be needed to carry out all the world's mathematical calculations, two men from Britain boarded a transatlantic liner. The men were on a mission, to find a way to automate the back-office processes of one of Britain's largest and most visible companies. They knew the best place to look: in unrationed, dynamic, business-oriented America, the home of IBM, they would find the machine solution they were seeking. It was the spring of 1947.

The tea shops of J. Lyons & Co. were unlikely pioneers of a computing revolution.

Cakewalk

The men were from J. Lyons & Co. Ltd, Britain's number one high-street catering company. Lyons were famous for their tea-shops on every corner – think Starbucks or Costa with tea rather than coffee – they manufactured the majority of their own products (Red Label tea, bread, cakes, ices,

sausages, ready-meals, you name it) and they were event caterers, wholesale food suppliers and more. The size, variety and complexity of the interacting operations of this company meant that armies of clerks were engaged in mind-numbing jobs – checking receipts, co-ordinating orders, managing logistics, analysing profits – and trying to get it done accurately and in time.

If ever there was a problem that needed to be mechanized, it was this. Unfortunately, the men from Lyons found that America had nothing to offer: they saw much equipment, many enthusiastic salesmen, IBM's punched-card machines and even the newly completed Pentagon. But nobody in the

The Pentagon building, the headquarters of the United States Department of Defense, soon found it needed computers.

Herman Goldstine, who had worked on ENIAC, met with the Lyons representatives and gave crucial advice to them on electronic computers.

USA seemed yet to grasp the needs of an already integrated, efficient, behind-the-scenes office management like the one Lyons had already built up over decades in the catering industry, providing low-margin sales in hundreds of outlets across an entire nation.

They were about to give up on the venture when they came across Herman H. Goldstine, the ENIAC engineer who had met John von Neumann on a railway platform and introduced him to the concept of electronic computation. The men from Lyons saw Goldstine in his university office at Princeton, where Goldstine was working on von Neumann's new computer project – bringing EDVAC into being. For the first time, the ideas that Lyons wanted to get across clicked: Goldstine was fascinated. He scribbled furiously on yellow pads, filling

them with his suggestions, explained about electronic computers and then revealed a most devastating piece of knowledge.

The whole trip to the USA had been a complete waste of time. For the man who could help Lyons with their problem was none other than Professor Douglas Hartree, a British computer scientist, who had just taken up the position of Professor of Mathematical Physics at Cambridge University. At Cambridge, they were building an electronic computing machine that might be just what the Lyons team were looking for. The central data-processing department of Lyons was located in west London – less than two hours away from Cambridge.

Back in England, Lyons approached Hartree and the man who really ran the computing show in Cambridge, Maurice Wilkes. The partnership was instantly

Douglas Hartree was working on building a computer at the University of Cambridge when the Lyons men came to know of him.

Princess Elizabeth, a few years before her coronation, was introduced to the LEO computer.

by business people, for business people.

The first royal encounter with a computing machine took place in early 1951, when HRH Princess Elizabeth was introduced to LEO. What she made of it is not recorded; it must have seemed a very strange tour as it took in choc-ice-making machinery and a device for the continuous manufacture of Swiss roll (the mind swirls), culminating in a demonstration of a huge jumble of hot electronics joined up to tubes full of mercury.

The LEO 1 computer, completed in 1951, was designed specifically for businesses.

made and cordial: Lyons would provide a financial contribution to Wilkes's research and would glean the benefits of Wilkes's experience for itself. Within a short while, though, it became apparent that what mathematicians needed from a computer differed significantly from that of a business user. The business machine should have a different specification – indeed, it should be developed specifically with businesses in mind. Lyons took a brave and remarkable step. They would build their own machine; it would not have some awful name like EDSAC or EDVAC or ENIAC, but the Lyons Electronic Office (LEO); and LEO computers would be a new business in its own right, providing specialist computing machines designed

Leo 1 Wally Dutton. 29/01/53

What made LEO different was the demands made on it by its users. Unlike EDSAC, it was not designed for complex mathematical calculations, so the design needed to be different.

States as well. When John Mauchly and Presper Eckert left the Moore School of Engineering in 1946, they established their own computer company: while they expected to get customers from among

Electronic calculators	Business computers
Mathematical operations are complex	At worst, we might need to multiply or divide something, or do a percentage, but we need to do lots of sorting
Limited number of variables but with hard-to-manage pieces like π, $\sqrt{-1}$ and exponents	Millions of variables, but all rather simple (nothing harder than the conversion of imperial units and pre-decimal currency into binary)
One-off computations	Routine reruns, with much data reused
Input and output devices can be offline and off the shelf as there will be post-run interpretation	Fast automated input and standardized printed outputs like pay-slips and invoices are essential
No deadline, we'll get to it when it's ready	Real-time processing is essential
Mathematics and numerical analysis	What about payroll and word processing and financial projections and invoicing and updating of reference data and...

LEO computers were effective – adopted by several industries and government ministries, such as Ford and the Met Office – but never a total commercial success. In part, this was because LEO was conceived by office systems experts and pushed along by boffins; a sales culture like that at IBM just did not exist in this milieu. It took until the third generation of LEO computers for the company to adopt the obvious logo of a regal lion and by then the company was close to being taken over.

Soon enough the idea of computing for business caught on in the United

mathematical users they also had an eye on the more general business community. Their machine was going to be called UNIVAC (Universal Automatic Computer), and their first customer, as with Herman Hollerith, was the US Census Bureau. Eckert and Mauchly's commercial venture was financially strained and in early 1950 their company merged with Remington Rand, which had a long track record in office machines like their iconic typewriters of a previous generation. UNIVAC mainframes became a major player in the American business computing market and it was only

A Packet for every Pocket

LYONS' TEA

Always the Best

COMPUTING WITH CAKE

A challenge for the Lyons Electronic Office was the long association in British minds of the Lyons brand with tea and cake. 'A potential computer user needs to have some confidence in his own judgment if he is to buy his computer from a teashop,' wrote the Office Management Association in 1955.

On the other side of the Atlantic one might be forgiven for thinking something similar. Remington, the promoter of UNIVAC computers, had diversified from typewriters in 1937, developing the electric shavers for which the brand name is still recognized. Just why might you buy a computer from a barber?

Over half a century things changed. Lyons teashops are no more, but their cake and biscuit brands (owned by different companies now) live on. Likewise Remington shavers, sold off in 1979, are still going strong. Neither product is now associated with computing machinery: LEO ended up (after a tortuous series of mergers) in what is now Fujitsu, and Remington Rand in Unisys.

Lyons was best known for its tea and cake. Rebranding it as a technology company was a significant challenge.

their success that forced IBM to recognize that they were behind in a race.

Foreign language

But the very different needs of business users of computers brought into the spotlight a central issue for the engineers and mathematicians who were trying to make electronic machinery carry out computing: how to make the machine do the special things that business users wanted. In other words, the problem of the program.

The early programs were horrible. A description of how the Manchester Mark I computer had to be programmed – admittedly one of the worst – gives the sense of it:

Each machine instruction consisted of 20 binary digits. An instruction was fed into the machine as four rows of holes/blanks on 5-track teleprinter tape, each row corresponding to a character on a teleprinter keyboard. Thus the written form of a program consisted of a sequence of 'words', each of four teleprinter characters. Unfortunately the characters corresponding to the 32 binary numbers 00000 ... 11111 were arranged in the entirely arbitrary sequence /E@A:SIU½DRJNFCKTZLWHYPQOBG2MXV£. Anyone who used the machine regularly ended up knowing this sequence by heart – I can still repeat it from memory. And this bizarre programming code was not the only complication facing a user. The Mark 1 had a C.R.T. [cathode ray tube] store, and in a C.R.T. store the trace always goes from left to right. So all numbers were stored and processed with the [least] significant digit on the left.

It's easy enough to snigger about this now, but in the pioneering days of computers each model was a scratch-built idiotype with its own special needs; and an efficient routine needed to take into account the limitations of the hardware, such as the discontinuous availability of data stored in delay-lines. Early programs called for immense attention to detail as well as mastery of the abstruse language of backwards teleprinter code. So the first computers came with their programs written by the computer engineers themselves and the computer designers were typically the computer users who wrote their own code for their own mathematical computations.

In 1949, America woke up to discover that the Soviet Union had exploded an atomic bomb. Suddenly, air defence against missiles flying over the North Pole seemed an urgent need. Sure, there were radar stations that could track self-propelled bombs, but by the time the data had been co-ordinated and assessed and the interceptor planes launched the bombs would have long since found their targets. A computerized system was needed. Using a computer built at MIT called Whirlwind – a rare example of an early computer with an attractive name – data received from radar were to be processed in real time to produce information rapidly enough for military commanders to take a decision. The system was called Semi-Automatic Ground Environment (SAGE). This gave rise to a range of new computing problems that required an awful lot of programming.

Evidently non-academic computer users had different needs from the mathematicians

The Cold War meant that defending against the threat of Soviet missiles was paramount. Radar systems were too slow and the calculations were too onerous to do by hand – a computerized system was needed. The Whirlwind, built by MIT, was the answer.

GOLD RUSH

The development of software for SAGE was entrusted to the Systems Development Division of the government-owned RAND Corporation, which had to implement a massive recruitment drive to get all the coders it needed for the project. (By 1959, SAGE was keeping 700 programmers and 1,400 other staff busy.) Such a large number of people suggested that a dedicated organization and premises were needed, so the Division became the System Development Corporation and moved to the orange-growing area of Santa Monica, CA. It wasn't 1849; the migrants were more genteel than the miners; but, as in the previous century, moving to California had its surprises and its promise of fortune. It was reckoned that the migration involved half the programmers of the United States. Since then, California's reputation as the Tech State has become unassailable. SAGE and oranges, a recipe for success.

The rush to the American west coast by technology firms began in the late 1950s. Santa Monica was the preferred location and drew coders, programmers and entrepreneurs enticed by the promise of riches, just like the gold rush a century before.

and, while outsourcing of programming to the computer company was feasible in the early stages, the diversity of needs meant that programming had to come in-house. If that was going to happen, the idiosyncrasies of different computing machines needed to be addressed: in other words, programming should have a common language. And then the machine would need to have the program translated for it into a sequence of machine-code instructions that it could follow according to the machine specifications of its manufacturer. The concept of the 'compiler' – and the languages to go with it – was born.

The mathematicians led the way on computer languages with something called the formula translator, or FORTRAN. Business computing, with its different needs, used common business-oriented language (COBOL) whose objectives were more directly practical and down-to-earth. A certain snobbery among academic computer scientists resisted the teaching of COBOL in

Grace Hopper was responsible for making the first compiler.

COMPILING WITHOUT SPELLING

Grace Hopper wrote the first American compiler. She generously claimed that she owed a debt to the book by Wheeler, Wilkes and Gill on programming and in particular to a library of their subroutines. For Hopper, the key point was the subroutines' standardized input and output. She coupled this concept with something she had picked up from John Mauchly, namely the 'short order code', which had codified algebraic ideas (such as variables and operations, like *a* or +) into binary. 'It was written in true algebraic format, but since there was no alpha, it didn't look very algebraic ... I think this was the first thing that clued me to the fact that you could use some kind of a code other than the actual machine code.'

She was also trying to acknowledge human nature. 'Programmers are lousy copyists! [It] was amazing how many times a 4 would turn into a delta which was our space symbol, or into an A ... And it therefore seemed sensible, instead of having programmers copy the subroutines, to have the computer copy the subroutines. Out of that came the A–0 compiler.' The reason it became called a compiler? The subroutines were in a library, and 'when you pull stuff out of a library you compile things'.

universities, despite the burgeoning growth of business computing in the second half of the 20th century. Despite this, COBOL's origins were thoroughly respectable: it was born out of a US Department of Defense meeting in the Pentagon in May 1959, when it was agreed that there should be a programming language that was in plain English (or nearly so), business-oriented, readable by laypeople, easily learned and compatible with all machines.

FORTRAN was one of a number of computer languages. More suited to academic uses, it was replaced by COBOL in business contexts.

HOLBERTON AND SAMMET

Among the many women who influenced the shape of business computing, two names stand out.

Betty Holberton (1917–2001) began her computing career as one of the programmers of ENIAC. She went on to work at Remington Rand and her 'Sort–Merge Generator', used for the 1950 US Census, was hailed by Grace Hopper as the thing that convinced her that computers could actually be used to write their own programs. In 1980, Holberton recalled the challenges of early computing: 'By 1951, engineers had well accepted the computer, but the business world was still very skeptical about it, because they had such questions as, "How do I know the data is on the magnetic tape?"' To convince those sceptics, she sprinkled iron filings on to computer memory tape and picked them up with sticky tape. You could 'see' the pulses of data with a magnifying glass. So there. Later in her career, Holberton developed COBOL and FORTRAN standards.

Betty Holberton (1917–2001) was one of the original programmers of ENIAC and played an important role in developing the FORTRAN and COBOL languages.

Jean E. Sammet (1928–2017) had a long career working for various companies, but spent most of her career at IBM. Having taught what may have been the first academic programming course at a higher education establishment, her interests were in theoretical computation – symbolic logic and manipulation of symbols, the subject at the very heart of programming. Sammet and Holberton were at the Pentagon meeting that kicked off the COBOL project. Sammet was the first woman to be elected president of the Association of Computing Machinery.

Software crisis

Snobbery, or the need for control, led to the phenomenon known as the 'software crisis' in the 1960s. The first programmers were a mix of men and women, a legacy of the war-era culture of joint working. By contrast, in post-war society men expected to get their pre-war jobs back, or be given new and more prestigious jobs, which created an undertow in which women might be swept away. Women as experts in computing did not easily fit into the post-war pattern and

in some cases women were deliberately held back and discriminated against. A wholly artificial result of this was that there were not enough programmers – that is to say, not enough male programmers – and the 'software crisis' was the result.

Pregnant programmers

The 'software crisis' provided opportunities for women programmers to get back in the game. On both sides of the Atlantic, enterprising women set up their own bureaux to which over-stretched clients could outsource their programming needs. In the US, Elsie Shutt had been forced by state laws to leave her job when she became pregnant. But that didn't apply to self-employed consultants, who could work on their own terms. Soon she had set up Computations, Inc., with a workforce of like-minded women working part-time who fitted coding in around their other activities. *Business Week* ran a piece in 1963 that cattily described the company as 'the pregnant programmers' – but the business model survived and thrived.

In the UK, Stephanie Shirley had a similar experience. Here it wasn't the law but employers' attitudes that pushed her into an entrepreneurial approach to computing. Repeated delays and excuses over her promotion in the Post Office (there had never been such a thing as a woman at the grade she would reach) drove her

out and life was no better in the private sector. So, like Elsie Shutt, she set up her own business, employing other women who were juggling home responsibilities with programming. Stephanie found it easier to win work by writing to prospective clients as 'Steve' Shirley and ran a tape-recording of typing sounds in the background at home to make it sound to callers like a more conventional workplace. Stephanie Shirley's business also succeeded and she was appointed DBE (Dame Commander of the Order of the British Empire) in 2000.

One effect of the software crisis – apart from the shortage of programmers – was the inability of projects to be completed on time and to budget. In part, this was because of the relative immaturity of the software industry, which only became separate from hardware manufacturing after IBM decided to 'unbundle' the two operations in 1970.

Wherever there is a gap in the market and the capital costs of starting an enterprise are low, entrepreneurs will swiftly move in. Software startups fitted this model perfectly and thousands of new enterprises sprang up, offering a wide range of products and services to businesses wanting to get more benefit from their computers. The services included processing (such as collection and input of punched cards, which continued as an input medium, or, later, magnetic tape, for uses such as payroll), time-sharing services and leasing of computers on behalf

Stephanie Shirley was driven out from the Post Office by a glass ceiling so she set up her own business, Freelance Programmers. She employed almost only women, to provide them with opportunities they could not find elsewhere.

of their owners to maximize the return on the hardware investment. Software products began with programs to help programmers, such as file-management systems and operating systems, but then moved in the 1970s towards applications that could be operated by end-users (clients) directly. Very often the startup would not need its own hardware, since the client would allow the hired expert to use its computer, without any real controls on how it was being used.

360-degree computing

Computer hardware (and a good deal of software) was, in the 1960s, still big and mainly sourced from IBM or one of its large competitors. The rise of IBM to dominate the computer market in the 1960s

---

GOING FOR BROKE

The Swinging Sixties are remembered for many things, but the Go-go dancer is one of the iconic emblems. The classic Go-go dancer is female, wears a miniskirt and has shiny knee-length boots made of white or bubblegum-coloured PVC. She dances in a disco on an elevated platform or, at the Whisky a Go Go nightclub on Sunset Strip in West Hollywood, in a cage.

The frenetic energy of Go-go lent its name to the behaviour of software stocks in the late 1960s. Some software companies went public in 1965 and 1966 and this began a frenzy of public listings and growth in prices of software stocks. By virtue of its position as a software provider, IBM found itself a beneficiary of this: 'In July [1968] the market valued I.B.M., whose physical assets amount to less than $6 billion, at more than $40 billion – more than any other company in the world, actually as much as the gross national product of Italy.' One software company's stock rose from $1.50 to $155 a share in under three years. People rushed to market: the software companies and the investors.

They called them the Go-go years. But it was a classic stock-market bubble, which burst when a recession began to bite in late 1969. Some companies folded, others were absorbed into larger competitors and some just soldiered on making losses rather than profits. Investors – including the software companies' original proprietors – lost their fortunes.

Go-going, going, gone.

As software stocks went public in the 1960s, their price just kept on rising. But like all stock market bubbles, the exuberance was short-lived.

IBM dominated the hardware industry, and the System/360 was a big reason why. Unlike its competitors, it could run programs written for a variety of machines.

was not inevitable. IBM had been slow to cotton on to the possibility that electronic computing machines might eat into its punched-card office machinery market, but once IBM was on to it, it made the space its own. Early IBM computers were stand-alone devices, as were all the others on the market. There was no idea of interoperability and even the possibility of running software designed for one machine on a different one was out of the question; so much for Alan Turing's idea of a 'universal' machine. But the game changed in 1964. IBM announced its System/360, which would double its revenues from computing.

System/360 looked just like other computers of the era: big, boring, rectangular steel boxes. But what made these boxes different was interoperability. The previous generation of computers demanded specifically created software for each machine: even IBM's own computers could not run programs written for another IBM machine. With System/360 all that would change. Everything would work with everything else. Customers could buy any number of units, with small or large processing power and up to 44 peripheral hardware components. The interconnections were standardized and programs would work with any of the different options. System/360 meant that customers could buy upgrades without having to rewrite their programs. It provided uniformity and at the same time flexibility. And it made IBM into the dominant player in the market for automated computing.

An instruction card for IBM's System/360.

SNOW WHITE

It may or may not be a myth that IBM sales staff were subject to a strict dress code, requiring them to be clean-shaven and wear a white shirt and a tie in all business settings. Apparently research showed that someone wearing a blue or yellow shirt was regarded as less professional.

It's debatable how strict IBM's rules were, or for how long they were in force, or whether they differed greatly from other business organizations. One thing, though, is certain. IBM's leading position in the market gave it a nickname. IBM was sometimes Big Blue, and sometimes Snow White, maybe in a surreptitious allusion to the dress code, and its competitors – Burroughs, CDC (Control Data Corporation), GE (General Electric), Honeywell, NCR (National Cash Register), RCA (Radio Corporation of America) and UNIVAC – were the Seven Dwarfs. Being large attracts lawsuits and insults. You're expected to perform at a super-human level, which means that shortcomings are more visible. IBM's software in the 1970s was widely thought mediocre: people bought it because it went with the machine, especially the System/360 machines, not because they liked it.

Q: What is an elephant?

A: A mouse with an IBM operating system.

Ouch. If you worked for IBM, you needed a thick skin under your white drip-dry nylon shirt.

IBM was known as 'Snow White' for its notorious policy of instructing its employees to wear plain white shirts and ties.

Being a dominant player may be great for profits in the short term, but modern economies prefer to have competition and sooner or later a large player is going to attract the attention of the authorities who police free and fair markets. In the earliest days, software was so integrated with hardware that software had been supplied free and IBM had continued the practice of providing a single package of computer and software – typically on a lease basis – for many years. Competition authorities do not like suppliers who 'bundle' products together because the single price ties in the customer to one product, squeezing out a potential competitor whose product may be better. Not surprisingly, given IBM's lead in the field, an investigation into the company was initiated by the US Department of Justice in 1967. This led to a decision by IBM to charge separately for five different services that had previously been bundled together into a single package. Software and programming were now separate from hardware. Curiously, the decision was liberating for IBM, not just because the

DoJ dropped the suit against IBM. The idea of an open standard, which enables pieces of hardware made by different manufacturers and software to be run regardless of the type of machine, is almost certainly a factor in the predominance of the 'IBM-compatible PC' in the post-1990s personal computer market.

By all accounts, the operating system supplied by IBM with System/360 – the virtual connector that should enable any software to run on whatever combination

---

IN THEIR SIGHTS

Competition authorities seem to target computer companies because of their size. Size, however, is not an offence: the issue is what you do with your dominant position, if you are successful enough to have one.

IBM's timely decision to unbundle called off the DoJ investigation in 1970. In 1967, IBM had 70 per cent of the United States' domestic computer market. In 1997, Microsoft products had 88 per cent of the market in personal computer operating systems. It was their turn, with a complaint that bundling their Internet Explorer web-browser with the Windows 95 operating system was anti-competitive vis-à-vis other browser products. Microsoft settled with the DoJ in 2001. That was not the end, because the EU Competition authorities had their go, this time reacting to complaints about the bundling of Windows with Windows Media Player and about enabling non-Microsoft networking software to be used to connect Windows-using desktops and servers. Microsoft was fined €497 million.

It goes on. Intel was ordered to pay a fine of €1,060 million in 2009 by the European Commission for making payments to computer manufacturers in order to dampen competition from other processor manufacturers, beginning a long series of appeals not yet resolved when this book went to press. In 2017, Google was fined €2,420 million for abusively exploiting its search-engine dominance to promote its own online shopping service.

Rank in Fortune 500 for year	1975	1985	1995	2005	2015
IBM	9	6	7	10	24
Apple		234	123	263	5
Microsoft			250	41	31
Amazon				303	29
Google					40

The competition enforcers have the benefit of hindsight, unlike investors. It is hard to predict winners and losers in the computer game. Apple was largely written off in the Nineties as little more than a niche interest. Microsoft wasn't an interesting company before Windows became the operating system of choice. A rise through the rankings – while the result of talent and savvy products – is rarely foreseeable.

HALL OF SHAME

The September 2005 issue of *IEEE Spectrum*, a magazine for the electrical and electronics industries, was devoted entirely to software project disasters and featured a full-page 'Hall of Shame' of over 30 failed or bungled software projects, including the following:

- 2005: Sainsbury's automated supply-chain management failed, leaving food going bad in warehouses, at an estimated cost of £290 million.
- 1996: An unmanned Ariane 5 space rocket blew up 40 seconds after launch at a cost of $500 million because a number that should have been expressed as an exponent had been treated as an integer and was too big for the system to handle.
- 1994: A Chemical Bank software error deducted $15 million from 100,000 customer accounts.
- 1979: North American Aerospace Defense Command falsely reported a full-scale Soviet Union attack, due to nothing more than a routine system test.

Back in the 1960s, the problems were classic project management ones, which the 2005 article happily listed: badly articulated project goals, immature technology, unrealistic budgeting, loose grip on change management, excessive ambition and complexity, bad communication and more. The story hasn't changed: in 2010 the US stock market lost $1 trillion, because of an automated trading algorithm that failed to correct as prices crashed.

The Ariane 5 space rocket exploded seconds after launch due to a software failure.

of System/360 machinery the customer had acquired – was too difficult to understand, debug and operate. But it showed the way forward. Automated computing was becoming accessible to a wider range of businesses. Manufacturers were beginning to think about the needs of medium-size firms as well as the huge pan-continental and international companies. Smaller 'mini-computers' came on to the market. The scope

and variety of business needs for computers was also causing the entrepreneurs to think about hardware again. But a transformative change came about only when downsizing the hardware was coupled with a wholly new approach to software.

It was the space age. The Apollo Guidance Computer accompanied the NASA missions to ensure the spacecraft remained on course: computers were now

NASA depends heavily on advanced computing technology to guide its spacecraft.

small and reliable enough to be sent into space, albeit with very simple and limited code. (It's said that on the Apollo 14 flight, the code had to be re-entered manually into the Apollo Guidance Computer and it took only 90 minutes to do so.) The computer had a horrible interface using switches and commands took the form of a verb (such as 'please perform' [code 50]) plus a noun (such as 'docking angles' [code 23]). Since the 1960s, more sophisticated computers have played a vital role in the success of space missions, with focus on reliability and long-term resilience to radiation levels experienced in space.

Easy and fun

Another lesson to be learned from the 'software crisis', if anyone had been attending, was that the industry was too internally focused. It was time to think outside the box and to ask what the customers

actually wanted. To get back to the days, 25 years before, when J. Lyons & Co Ltd had started with a problem and asked for a computing solution.

The chief issue with the computers of the first 20 or so years was not that they were big, expensive capital investments or that they were temperamental: it was that they required specialists to operate them. Business leaders do not have the time to become specialists; nor do middle-managers, the people on whom the leaders depend for their information and to execute the company's policy. To call for more coders was not the solution. What was needed was

---

BURN, BABY, BURN

When the Apollo Guidance Computer's code became publicly available, it revealed some interesting things, none of them about space flight. Instructions are labelled 'trashy little subroutines' and 'numero mysterioso', there are quotes from Shakespeare and an instruction for moving the radar antenna that tells the astronauts to 'crank the silly thing around'. Among the jokes hidden in the code is a throwback to the 1965 Los Angeles riots, a catch-phrase that was used for really hot records by disc-jockey Magnificent Montague. The Apollo 11 routine for ignition of its rockets is entitled 'BURN_BABY_BURN-MASTER_IGNITION_ROUTINE'.

ARQMAQ

The sight of senior armed-services personnel decked out in full uniform on a university campus is, perhaps, unusual. A visit to a funded programme of research may be what is going on; but one thing you can be sure of is that the generals and admirals are not going to be visiting the Architecture Department. Unless the university is MIT and the year is 1976.

For MIT's Architecture Machine Group had grown beyond the simple idea of computer-aided building design and had translated its ideas about making computers 'easy and fun to use' into a full-on research project. Understanding that front-line forces do not have the time to fuss about with coding on the battlefield, the Group obtained funding from the Defense Advanced Research Projects Agency (ARPA) to develop those ideas.

The Architecture Machine Group (nicknamed Arqmaq by its go-ahead coders – the lab's visionary professor, Nicholas Negroponte, was grumpy about that) brought in people from a range of backgrounds and disciplines, spinning out ideas that wowed the generals and set the agenda for computer development – or rather, the 'man-machine interface' – for the next two decades. Pioneering developments included a voice-activated pointer that navigated around a 'desktop' displaying various icons, representing different functions such as the telephone or document filing system or calculator or whatever. There was also a three-dimensional moving map of Aspen, Colorado and the unheard-of notion that on-screen text might actually be presented in attractive fonts rather than computer script.

There were also touch-sensitive TV displays. This was so counter-intuitive in the 1970s that, in the lab, the catchphrase was 'touch the screen, bozo'. One hopes nobody said 'bozo' to a general.

Nicholas Negroponte headed MIT's Architecture Machine Group, which was responsible for creating a number of exciting projects, ranging from touch-screen TVs to the 3D Aspen Movie Map.

computing that was easy for non-specialists to do – people like managers, the ones on the front line.

To facilitate this, two things were needed: an innovative approach to the way in which people used computers and to have pre-packaged programs that business people could deploy out of the box. In fact, what was needed was not so much 'programs' as products. Products that would provide an instant solution to a business need: for financial forecasting, or for word-

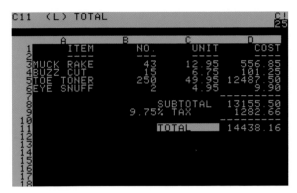

```
C11  (L) TOTAL                              C
                                            25
        A       B         C         D
    1        ITEM     NO.      UNIT     COST
    2
    3 MUCK RAKE       43     12.95    556.85
    4 BUZZ CUT        15      6.75    101.25
    5 TOE TONER      250     49.95  12487.50
    6 EYE SNUFF        2      4.95      9.90
    7
    8                    SUBTOTAL   13155.50
    9        9.75% TAX               1282.66
   10
   11                    TOTAL      14438.16
   12
   13
   14
   15
   16
   17
   18
```

Visicalc may not have been much to look at, but the world's first electronic spreadsheet brought computers to a much wider audience.

processing, or for data sorting.

The first electronic spreadsheet computer program, VisiCalc, which hit the market in 1979, did exactly what the name said. VisiCalc was produced by VisiCorp for the Apple II computer (see page 141). On the terminal screen of the computer, VisiCalc would set out an array of figures, just as you might painstakingly set out on ruled accounting paper, with columns for months or branches and so forth and rows for prices or volumes of sales or other variables. VisiCalc allowed you to change one variable and automatically all the other dependent figures would change to reflect the difference. Gone were the days of having to erase all the numbers and redo all the sums with a pocket calculator and remember which ones were functions of what and re-redo the sums when you realized that a changed assumption affected other data you were processing. Better still, VisiCalc had it all laid out before you on the screen. Type in the new figure and the screen would refresh with a neatly redone

chart. With VisiCalc, business planning actually became about planning; it became fun. It also made its developers, Dan Bricklin and Bob Frankston, a lot of money.

New software products were an essential part of making computers easier to use. So was miniaturization. Small (tiny, compared with the megaliths of the 1960s) computers came on to the market in the 1970s, priced at a level small businesses could afford. Suddenly, computing was within touching distance of everybody, except that not everybody needed to run a spreadsheet. What it would take to bring computing into every home was a revolution and that revolution would start not in the computing industry but in the high street.

Dan Bricklin developed Visicalc with Bob Frankston while still at Harvard Business School.

Chapter 7

SIZE MATTERS

Although technology had developed so that computers could become smaller, the computer industry saw little need for 'personal' computers. That changed when improved graphics, family-friendly products and the Internet became available, almost all at once. The mouse, the graphical operating system made famous by Apple computers, and electronic mail all became indispensable. The growth of the Internet led to the dot.com boom and bust, and the recharacterization of computers as pieces of communications technology.

For computers to reach the wider public, they would need to become much smaller. Miniaturization would be the goal for decades to come.

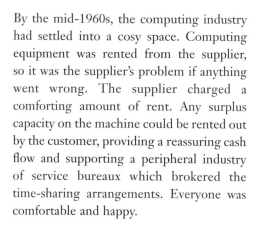

By the mid-1960s, the computing industry had settled into a cosy space. Computing equipment was rented from the supplier, so it was the supplier's problem if anything went wrong. The supplier charged a comforting amount of rent. Any surplus capacity on the machine could be rented out by the customer, providing a reassuring cash flow and supporting a peripheral industry of service bureaux which brokered the time-sharing arrangements. Everyone was comfortable and happy.

Consumers in the driving seat

Any radical change was therefore going to come from outside. Take transistors, for example. These had been invented at (there's a pattern here) Bell Labs in 1947, but there was little drive to replace big, hot, power-hungry, fragile valves with smaller, unreliable, expensive components like transistors. The changeover was slow and only happened when the cost of a transistor fell sufficiently. But transistors had caught the eye of other industries, especially those

John McCarthy (1927–2011) was one of the founding fathers of artificial intelligence.

JOHN McCARTHY

The name of John McCarthy (1927–2011) deserves greater recognition in the story of computing. He's known as one of the founding fathers of artificial intelligence, having organized the conference at Dartmouth, New Hampshire, in 1956, when the subject was first launched as a research discipline. He also worked on computer languages (notably Lisp) and developed a chess-playing algorithm.

But one enduring thing that McCarthy started was hidden from view, yet radically changed the way computers can be used. The capacity of a mainframe is rarely fully utilized if it is serving a single program only: at its simplest, the computer would be sitting idle while a user put in a program or the associated data. Using computers was a lumpy business, with a user having a burst of activity followed by a period of relative non-use. With an expensive piece of hardware and lots of demand, a more efficient model was needed.

McCarthy implemented the first time-sharing system at MIT in 1959. This allowed multiple users to use the same machine at the same time, with the computer itself keeping track of where each user was in their own routines. Indirectly, this meant that people could access the computer remotely via a terminal and in due course direct interaction with the machine did away with off-line programming with punched cards or tape.

While, these days, many of us don't use mainframes directly, time-sharing is still with us: any multi-user system, such as a server handling a network, or the ubiquitous Cloud, needs to make use of a derivative of McCarthy's concepts.

Transistors replaced valves as the essential component of computers due to their reliability and small footprint.

like valves, they can also amplify the signal.

Then came the idea of using a slice or 'chip' of semi-conductor material integrated with tiny transistors to house complete circuits, so that the chip itself included small-scale computing power. It became possible to great-ly miniaturize electronic components to make devices that were not only smaller but also much more powerful than the old valve-driven ones. Hearing aids could be smarter and other possibilities – like digital watches and electronic calculators – became feasible and they sold. The integrated circuit was just one step away from a fully programmable chip.

manufacturing consumer products.

During the inter-war years and after, every household had its wireless. But think of the sales possibilities if you could have a wireless in your car! This became possible in the late 1950s, when transistors had proved that they could do the job of valves, but more resiliently and more compactly, which facilitated miniaturization. Consumer demand supported other down-sized products too, such as hearing aids.

The valves used in early electronic components were called 'valves' for a good reason: as with the valves that control water flow, the fluid medium in electronics – electricity – can flow one way through a valve but not the other. Valves could also be engineered, by adding a third electrode, to amplify the signal flowing through them. Elements such as germanium and silicon can behave like valves, passing current one way only. They are therefore called semiconductors. In the right conditions,

Silicon was the essential ingredient in the recipe for smaller computers.

DEATHNIUM

It does not follow that a new technology will immediately oust an old one. Manufacturing semiconductors with the right properties was, initially, very hard and getting rid of impurities was hardest of all. One unwanted ingredient of early transistors was 'deathnium': its chemical origins unknown back then, but its property of killing transistors notorious. (It turned out to be copper.) These days, computer chips are prepared in ultra-clean labs where there is zero tolerance for any worker who brings in the tiniest speck of something foreign.

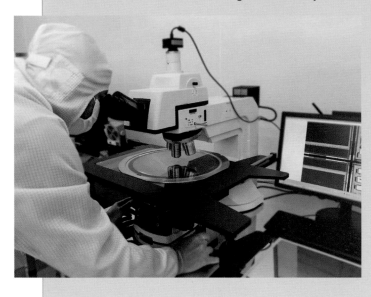

Manufacturing semiconductor chips is a delicate process. Today, they are prepared in sterile laboratories free from impurities.

Calculator

Electronic calculators – handheld battery-powered machines that would do very basic arithmetic – first became available in shops in the early 1970s. There was immediately a big and enduring fuss about whether students should be allowed to use them, probably because 'if I had to do it the hard way then so should you'. By the end of the decade, calculators had become 'scientific' because their processors allowed for a range of trigonometric and statistical functions and were even 'programmable'. After 50 years, the portable calculator, whose menial job is that old, old problem in computing – to improve accuracy in simple arithmetic – has enjoyed an unpredictable persistence. Even

though there is a calculator app on your phone or your desktop, who does not find it helpful to use a stand-alone calculator from time to time, either at home or at work?

Electronics had made things smaller. Smaller, more compact, more flexible, more portable. But what were the implications for computing? The answer was: not much, until the development of the microprocessor. Before the microprocessor, there were integrated circuits and printed circuit boards, which still had to be wired together to obtain the full functionality of a computer. A microprocessor was what it said: the whole of a computer's processing unit shrunk on to a chip.

Handheld calculators emerged in the 1970s and they continue to survive to the present day, even as desktop and phone apps copy their functionality

OR and arithmetical operations, a control section and its own memory (the 'cache'). Different designs may be appropriate for graphics processing, machine controllers, mobile phones and so forth.

Efficient microprocessing is dependent on efficient microprogramming. In the mid-1970s a research programme funded by the US Defense Advanced Research Projects Agency led to the development of RISC, reduced-instruction-set computing. Keeping things simple (the 1982 RISC-1 processor had only 32 instructions) paradoxically speeded things up and informed chip design.

Microprocessors are the tiny power-houses of modern computers. Rather than being straightforward assemblies of transistors lined up on a chip, they are tiny computers in their own right. Miniaturization allowed the configuration of elements on a chip so that they could be connected together internally, rather than using an old-fashioned circuit board. As with macro computer design, how the pieces are put together is driven by the tasks that the microprocessor is intended to perform; typically, there will be an operational section doing Boolean-logical activities such as AND and

It was not just happening in the rarefied environs of academic laboratories. In the 1970s, industrial manufacturers began to produce microprocessors for use by computer companies. Since their invention, microprocessors have become pervasive: not just in the design of computers, but embedded in cars and household devices such as washing machines.

Microprocessors contain a computer's entire processing power on a single chip. The RISC processor shown here, with its limited instruction set, made programming far more efficient.

INTEL™ v. AMD

Intel was founded in 1968 by Gordon Moore (of Moore's law fame, see opposite) and Robert Noyce, a physicist expert in integrated circuits. Intel's success was built out of a happy coincidence: its line of microprocessors was available just at the moment when 'personal computers' were taking off. Intel's x86 (and later Pentium) processors powered the first generation of home computers enjoyed by millions of families.

Intel has dominated the microprocessor market since its inception in 1968.

The Intel logo is a registered trademark of the Intel Corporation.

Intel's major competitor is AMD, which has always had a smaller market share. AMD's breakthrough was in having read-only memory embedded on its chips and since then its focus has been to create low-wattage processors suitable for battery-powered devices such as handheld devices and consoles. In 2006, AMD acquired ATI with its graphics card, containing an embedded microprocessor that could process graphics without needing to access the computer's central processing unit. Compactness and frugality.

As with other giants in the tech industry, AMD and Intel have had their agreements (notably a deal for sharing intellectual property in the 1980s) and their lawsuits (a case between them began in 2005 and was settled four years later, but as the larger market player Intel has been on the receiving end of several investigations and actions from the competition authorities).

As to tablet computers, the flat modular computers with touchscreen LCD display that fill a niche somewhere between laptops and smartphones, neither AMD nor Intel has much impact. Here the entire system is on a chip and those chips are typically made by Arm Holdings, based in Cambridge, UK.

Gordon Moore, the founder of Intel, has had a successful and long-lasting career in the technology industry.

When cheap, mass-produced chip-based processors became available in the 1970s, those huge racks of hardware could finally be sent for recycling. The first microprocessors had rather limited functionality and low speed, so their use was primarily for calculators and simple control systems. Inevitably – or so it seems – more computing power became concentrated into a single chip and that meant that the thing that was once no better than a calculator was now strong enough to tackle modern computing tasks.

By the late 1970s, the consumer electronics industry had fostered a wealth of exciting products that had very little, if anything, to do with computing. It was, however, a marriage of the values and

attractive presentation of a consumer-orientated business with the most traditional of computer companies that would create a market for a new type of computer: the personal computer.

Although computers had been coming down in size, from the warehouse-filling hunks of soldered engineering of the 1950s

THE LAWS OF PROCESSING

In the 1960s, Walter F. Bauer, the entrepreneur behind Informatics Inc., formulated a couple of laws. Bauer's first law was: 'If the program has a bug, the computer will find it.' Interesting, but it didn't catch on – probably because Bauer's 'laws' were formulated to stimulate interest in his company, rather than state a scientific proposition.

But in the 1965, Moore's 'law' was proposed and it stuck. Gordon Moore made a prediction that he never intended to be treated as a 'law' like those for gravity or thermodynamics. While it's observable it is not provable and it may have a finite lifespan. Moore's original prediction was that the number of components that could be placed on a chip would approximately double each year. Subsequently the doubling-time was extended to something between one and two years, but in the first 50 years since Moore made his prediction it has held up remarkably well. In due time, though, the number of components will be constrained by the number of atoms on a chip – unless at that moment effective quantum computing becomes possible.

Bauer's second law was that talent migrates to areas of expanding activity. Dr Bauer's company was absorbed into the company now called CA Technologies, which, as one of the world's largest software companies, has held up well too; maybe there was something in his laws after all.

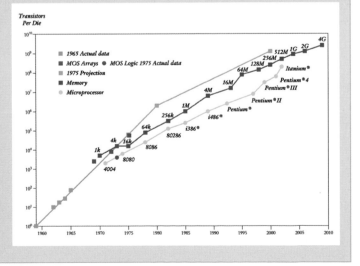

Moore's law forecasted that the transistor count, and therefore the processing power, of microprocessors would double every year.

ALTAIR 8800

The Altair 8800 do-it-yourself personal computer kit has a revered place in computing history. According to legend, the appearance of this thing on the cover page of *Popular Electronics* in 1975 is what began the personal computer revolution.

Sadly the facts are less impressive than the legend. The Altair 8800 was not going to compete with any business computer of its era, nor was it capable of doing any really serious computing at all. The Altair came with only 256 bytes of memory, which Paul Allen, co-founder of Microsoft, says was 'just enough to program its lights to blink'.

What the Altair 8800 could do, without doubt, was to inspire. It not only brought computers into people's homes – admittedly homes that included nerdy electronics hobbyists – but it indicated a possible future. And that vision of a future captured the imaginations of two such nerds, Paul Allen and Bill Gates, who saw in the tiny potential of this useless machine the foundation for a business that ultimately became Microsoft.

The Altair 8800 brought computing into people's homes even if it could not compete in speed or power with the business computers of its day.

to the mini-computers of the 1970s, the idea of a small, single-person computer was self-evidently something that would never catch on.

It was really about what you thought computers were for. Universities and other researchers needed computing power to run computer models. Things had moved on from the notion that one computer could calculate all the missile trajectories you could think of, but calculations remain at the heart of research computing.

As to businesses, there was equally no obvious need for a small computer. A medium-size business could rent computing time on a large mainframe and there were service providers to help that happen. The marketplace was competitive, with a healthy effect on prices. Why would small stand-alone machines be of benefit to anyone?

And the most extreme case of absurdity was the household. What conceivable use could a family have for a computing machine?

The PDP-11 produced by the Digital Equipment Corporation in the 1970s was one of its incredibly popular 'minicomputers'.

The personal computer came together because of a happy coincidence of three things:

• The electronic components of computers had become miniaturized and, importantly, cheaply reproducible. Processor chips mass-produced in factories packaged unprecedented computing power into a small box – if only there were a market for such devices.

• The idea that families did not want to spend their lives managing domestic finances with spreadsheets took a long time to die. For many years it was assumed that the reason a family would buy a computer was to do at home the kind of thing that businesses did with them. Wrong. The

reason people bought computers was to play games: things people do at home are different from the things they do in the office. Once games became computerized, the market was there.

• The most important thing of all was the graphical user interface (GUI). Business computers still depended heavily on punched cards or tape for input and reams of fan-folded paper PRINTED IN UNREADABLE USER-UNFRIENDLY UPPER-CASE LETTERS IN TELEX

The Honeywell Kitchen Computer from 1969 reflected the desperate attempts to get computers into the home. Costing $10,000 and requiring a two-week course in binary, it never caught on.

PONG

The transformation of computing owes something to the emergence of the video-games industry in the late 1970s and early 1980s. Bars in the early 1970s had pinball machines and slot machines to amuse the customers. Then, in 1972, a new machine was installed in a bar in California: it had a primitive video table-tennis game with the single instruction 'Avoid missing ball for high score'. Within 48 hours the machine had broken down – not a great start for the video games industry. Then the engineer opened the machine and found it was still working perfectly; the problem was that the coin box was overflowing and the chute from the coin-slot was entirely clogged with quarter-dollars. The super-successful prototype with the overflowing coin box was called 'Pong'.

The Pong craze overtook America in the late 1970s. The primitive tennis game replaced pinball machines as the favourite attraction of bars and arcades and showed people that computers could be used for fun as well as work.

FONT for output. The development of the visual display unit meant that the computer could look like that most attractive of all consumer electronic devices, the television.

The Computer Revolution was bound up with the idea that using the machine should be an intuitive, user-oriented experience. The big problem with computers of a previous generation was the clunky way that humans communicated with the machine. The QWERTY keyboard was something understood only by secretaries and the presentation of information on dingy screens with monochrome green script was obscure and unwelcoming. Printout on long screeds of fanfold paper looked boring, even for those who had to study it.

The 'graphical user interface' changed that. Graphics made computer screens more interesting to look at. Graphics are things you point at. So when the mouse made it possible to point and click, the GUI made it possible for a new range of computer applications, designed around a new breed of user, to come on to the market. Once you no longer needed specialist skills to use a computer, anyone could use them and everyone did.

The place that televisions occupy in the history of computing is rarely mentioned. Televisions have for many years been on the periphery of computing, providing an interface, or a channel for communication. Televisions can now be rigged as computer monitors and computers can be rigged to receive TV, but there has been a reluctance to achieve complete merger between similar technologies. Yet the shared history is informative: games consoles were plugged into TV displays; before the Internet, TV was a (somewhat unloved, but useful) medium for search and delivery of information; and hardware developments have fed across from one industry to the other. The invention of the liquid crystal display (LCD) in 1964, for example, made flat-screen TV possible, later used in personal computers. It is not an accident that televisions and computers look similar.

The fact that accessing the output of a computer via a screen was not developed until the 1970s is an indication of what

MODEL

Computer modelling is everywhere. Mathematicians have for generations represented behaviours they observe in the real world in the form of equations; computerization just takes this one stage further. Instead of laboriously crunching the solutions to equations in the old way, the computer can take over, enabling more complex multi-variable interdependent models to be created. Unpredictable things like the weather can become more understandable.

Computer modelling may have begun with Alan Turing's venture in 1952 into the development of shape and form in living things, which he was able to predict using differential equations run on the Manchester Mark I computer to create an early form of heat-map. More modern applications study car crashes, flight simulation, the behaviour of astronomical bodies and finance.

Computers could now be used to model real world phenomena. The weather, in theory, would be much better understood once computers were used to model it.

135

CEEFAX, MINITEL AND PRESTEL

In 1972 the BBC started a new 'teletext' service, called Ceefax. Information could be delivered to your TV screen, outside the normal schedule of broadcasts. Although it was slow to use (you had first to find the page number where the information you wanted was displayed, and then wait for it to scroll through all the other pages until it got to the one you had selected) and its graphics were very simple, it provided an up-to-date way to find out sports results, weather forecasts, travel information and news headlines, without needing special equipment. Other broadcasters, such as ITV's ORACLE, offered similar services.

In France, they went one better. Minitel was an interactive service operated over a phone line and it was much closer in user experience to a full Internet service. As well as news and information, Minitel had online shopping, train reservations and mail. Unlike Ceefax, to have Minitel you needed a terminal – but that didn't seem to put off the consumers. Nine million terminals were installed, giving a prototype form of Internet access to 40 per cent of the population. The UK Post Office started a similar service called Prestel in 1979. It required a special television and dedicated phone line and never achieved the success of Minitel. It ended in 1994, just as the Internet was starting to develop. Both Minitel and Ceefax finally died in 2012, when TV signals went digital and the analogue signal was switched off, having survived the real Internet era for a surprisingly long time.

Ceefax was the BBC's 'teletext' service, which could broadcast information to the TV screen, including weather forecasts, sports results, travel information and more.

people thought computers were for. Back in the days of ENIAC, blinking lights on the units were there to tell the engineers whether all was well inside the machine, not to produce the output of a program. (Ping-pong balls were cut in half and glued over the lights with numbers on them to indicate what was happening during the machine's run.) The association of computers with arithmetic – and with a numerical, or, grudgingly, alpha-numerical, printout – was from the outset hard to shake. However,

beginning with VisiCalc, developers of computer programs recognized that non-specialist users needed something more accessible.

Wang Laboratories was not a computer company at all. It started out making electronic calculators and only diversified into computing in the 1970s, beginning with word processors. Initially, word processors were glorified typewriters, showing a few lines of text that were potentially modifiable before the print-head did its stuff. The

Computers were now small enough to place on a desk and showed a visual output, rather than a punched card. Companies like Intel made the most of this in their advertisements.

important thing was that there was a visual display; the next step was a display of the whole document, enabling chunks of text to be moved around and for other operations, which are either very difficult or unimaginable with a typewriter, to take place. Wang first produced a visual display unit (VDU)-based word processing program in 1976.

The computing revolution

Everyone knows that the fall of the Berlin Wall in 1989 symbolized the anti-Communist revolution that swept across Europe in the last years of that decade. In the world of computing, another, perhaps equally significant, revolution, was also taking place. Three big ideas had come to fruition at much the same time:

• At last, computers had become easy and fun to use. No longer did you have to have specialist training or to be an 'expert' to be able to operate a computer. The big difference was an operating system that didn't require typing skills and understanding of obscure 'C:\>' symbols in order to run a piece of software: now

it was intuitive, using a mouse-click and pointer to activate an icon on the screen.

• User-orientated computers appeared on office desks everywhere. These not only helped non-specialists become familiar with computers but also allowed them to communicate with their colleagues and, after a while, other business contacts, using email. Quite soon, memos, paperwork and dictaphones became redundant. Only the office dinosaur needed his emails printed out by his secretary.

• Computers became powerful sources of information. They provided access to something called the World Wide Web, which enabled every business, every government agency and even private citizens to set up a shop window that told the world – anyone who wanted to visit their site – whatever they wanted. The Internet was born.

Windows

Once the visual display idea had caught on – once it had proved itself as the way in which money was to be made – the shape of the computer as we currently know it was settled. The computer terminal needed more than an alpha-numeric keyboard for input and a printer for output: it needed a visual display for real-time monitoring of the application to which the computer was being put. Gone were the days of feeding in punched tape, typing 'run' and waiting for the printer to chunter out pages of paper to be pored over later. Now computing would be done in front of a screen; and that screen might not be a terminal at all, but a self-contained micro-computer not connected to anything but the electricity supply.

There was, however, a challenge. Computer users might need to use more than one application at a time. Say you are writing a report that needs figures. Halfway through the report it dawns on you that the reader might need an alternative projection of the figures, which came out of a spreadsheet program. To continue with the report, the spreadsheet needs to be rerun. The traditional way to solve the problem was to save your work on to a floppy disk, exit the program, load (via another floppy disk) whatever software was needed for the spreadsheet program, rerun the data, save and print the results, exit the spreadsheet program, reload the word-processor program, and so on. Large-memory computers might allow you to store the programs inside the machine, but the exit-and-restart problem was still there, even with clever operating systems like the hugely successful MS-DOS developed by Microsoft in the years before it was famous.

DOS

In the summer of 1975, Bill Gates and Paul Allen founded a company called 'Micro-Soft'. The timing was perfect: the personal computer was just taking off. Initially, Micro-Soft produced a compiler that enabled inexpert programmers using the introductory language BASIC to program a microcomputer such as the Altair 8800 and a generation of more sophisticated machines then being developed, in particular by IBM.

IBM invited Microsoft (now without

With a new audience, an easier method of accessing programs was needed. Along came Microsoft Windows, an operating system that solved the exit-and-restart problem.

the hyphen) to develop an operating system for the microcomputer it was developing in 1980. With a deft acquisition and retooling of an operating system product they were able to provide MS-DOS (Microsoft Disk Operating System) to IBM. By 1983, according to the historian Martin Campbell-Kelly, nearly a million IBM-compatible PCs had been sold and 90 per cent were running MS-DOS.

DOS was something for the geeks, not for ordinary folk. On the black screen were displayed the mysterious symbols C:\>_ with the underscore flashing menacingly: you had to give it a command and if you got it wrong the machine would crash. But at the time, MS-DOS was where it was at; running in the background, it was making enough money for Microsoft to enable them to move to the next level, to develop a range of applications to run on their operating system and to produce the next iteration of operating system, known as 'Windows'.

Paul Allen says it wasn't even called 'Windows' when it was in development – the product was originally going to be called

'Interface Manager'. Not as bad a name as VisiCalc, but better than DOS even if not as homely as Windows.

Ultimately, though, what made Microsoft the leading name in software was the combination of Windows with a package of office software, including word processing, slide shows, spreadsheets and email. Some versions of the Microsoft Office suite did not endear the company to its customers: an unintended side-effect of the 'Office Assistant' was to cause users to swear loudly at the intrusion of a chirpy paper-clip offering help with letter-writing as soon as one typed the word 'Dear' in a document.

Microsoft was the company founded by Bill Gates and Paul Allen, who started working together in 1971, with a system to analyse data collected by traffic sensors in the city of Seattle, WA. They planned to market it under the brand name Traf-O-Data. It's no surprise that Traf-O-Data was a flop, but what Gates and Allen had learned was a great deal about how a microprocessor could be used as a full-function computer. When Intel produced a much more powerful microprocessor, the 8008, in 1975, Gates and Allen saw an opening. That do-it-yourself Altair 8800 machine could only be programmed in machine language – but Gates and Allen wrote a compiler that would enable enthusiasts to program it in BASIC and the foundation of Microsoft was laid. The company's first business line was the supply of programming languages to the microcomputer industry.

Microsoft's close relationship with IBM,

WORKING IN PAIRS

Many of the success stories in modern computing have been the product of partnerships.

Bill Gates and Paul Allen started Microsoft in 1975. They had met at high school only a few years before. While they shared a passion for programming, their successful company was the result of combining complementary skills, with Gates focusing on marketing and growth, and Allen coming up with ideas.

Steve Jobs and Steve Wozniak were the duo behind Apple. Again, they were high school friends, and Jobs's presentational skills filled out the design capabilities of Wozniak.

Gordon Moore and Robert Noyce founded Intel. They were both scientists, and a third member of the team, Andy Grove, also had a science background and later became the company's leading commercial force.

Other examples abound. Even IBM, widely regarded as the creation of Thomas J. Watson, Sr, was a partnership of Watson's commercial drive and the inventiveness of Herman Hollerith. It's rarely the case that a single name is behind success.

Bill Gates launched Microsoft with Paul Allen in 1975. He was the business mind behind the venture, while Allen was responsible for the technical side – a partnership reflected in many tech companies.

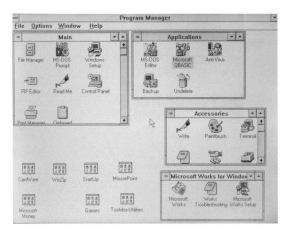

Windows 3.1 was far easier to use than MS-DOS, which had preceded it.

together with IBM's open structure of compatible devices and software, enabled the development of a visual operating system that allowed users to switch between applications – indeed to have several running at the same time, in different 'windows'. Heavily influenced by developments at Xerox and Apple, Microsoft's Windows system was launched in November 1985. It wasn't the only entrant into the market, but it was cheaper than the others, it was announced with lots of coloured razzmatazz, it worked on the tried-and-trusted MS-DOS foundation and it was compatible with lots of machines and – most important of all – the partnership with IBM provided a solid basis from which to sort out the glitches and develop a really effective platform. There was only one thing wrong with it: it looked and felt like a rip-off of Apple's Macintosh machine.

Apple revolutionized the personal computer by including a graphical user interface.

The revolutionary Mac

The launch of Apple's Macintosh computer was the computing revolution equivalent to the fall of the Bastille. In one compact plastic box, Apple combined a small screen, a graphical user interface, which used a mouse for commands, and ready-loaded software. Computer geeks grumbled that this simple package took the mystique out of computing, but that was exactly the point. When you switched it on, a square-ish happy face, something like a cross between a computer screen and a smiley, greeted you. It was corny, but it was fun and easy to use. And there were no wires – most people hate the untidy electronic knitting that seems to be necessary with a new computer. In the UK they were even powered by the same plug leads used for kettles, and just like a kettle, you could plug the Apple Mac in and expect it to boil.

The origins of the Apple Computer Company are the stuff of legend. Steve

BIG MAC LOGO

It's sometimes asked whether Apple designed its logo in commemoration of the tragic death of Alan Turing. Turing died in 1954 after taking a dose of cyanide and a partly eaten apple was found by his bedside.

The bite in the Apple logo was not, in fact, a reference to Alan Turing's suicide, but instead was used to distinguish it from a cherry.

It seems, however, that the truth is rather more prosaic. Various 'apple' motifs were offered to Steve Jobs, the company's founder, for his approval. The bite was taken out of the side to give it scale, because Jobs thought there was a risk people could mistake the logo for a cherry, which would rather miss the point. The rainbow colours were to demonstrate the capabilities of the computer, not to recognise Alan Turing's LGBT status. But they did come up with the slogan 'Byte into an Apple'.

All right, but what has all that got to do with the Mac? The initiator of the Apple computer project, Jef Raskin, wanted to name his new easy-to-use design after his favourite type of apple. That happened to be a McIntosh, but there was a computer company of that name, so the computer morphed into Macintosh and over time to just Mac. Imagine, your favourite computer could have been named Granny Smith and wouldn't that be a happy meal.

Wozniak and Steve Jobs used to go to the Homebrew Computer Club, a group of enthusiasts in Menlo Park, CA, in the mid-1970s. The clunky Altair – which had no input other than switches and no output other than flashing lights – had caught the imagination of Wozniak, who thought that a simple, cheap computer should have a keyboard and a visual display, like a typewriter and a television. The idea of the Apple I computer was born and the first units were assembled by hand, as the legend has it, in a garage. The Apple II was much more sophisticated, with colour graphics and magnetic tape as external memory and it was much more expensive. However, what really made the Apple II a success was the VisiCalc application, which put Apple Computers firmly on the map. Yet the Apple II was still a traditional-style machine, with input via the keyboard and with output in the form of lines of text, albeit on the screen. What the Mac promised was to change all that.

The Apple Mac didn't sell too well, because its memory capacity and range of applications were too limited for business use. But the principles it embodied were noted by competitors, notably those making IBM-compatible machines. Apple had set a new standard of ease of use that everyone now expected.

Apple's philosophy was like a revolution in customer relations. The computer had discovered that it should serve its user, rather than have its user change to fit the idiosyncrasies of the machine (although some present-day computer users would dispute this assertion). That, one might naïvely imagine, would give Apple and its Macintosh range an irresistible surge of demand, assuring them dominance in the market. However, the adoption of Windows by manufacturers of IBM-compatible personal computers re-created the same ideals of user service.

Perhaps, given that background, it might be a surprise that the best-selling lines of personal computers were neither Apples nor IBM products.

- It is said that 12.5 million units of the Commodore 64 were sold, making it the best-selling personal computer of all time. This popular machine, dating from 1982, could be plugged in and used at once, though it lacked the user-orientated features of the Apple Mac. It was also cheap ($600), putting it in reach of home buyers. But its big selling point was probably the games packages that came with the machine.

- The Sinclair Spectrum ZX80, introduced in 1980, was the cheapest computer in the UK at under £100. It was the UK equivalent of the Commodore in introducing British people to computers. The ZX Spectrum, introduced in 1982, was the UK's best-selling personal computer, outselling Commodore and Amstrad.

- Small businesses also needed cheap, easy-to-use computers and they flocked to a machine that had a graphical interface not dissimilar to that of the Apple. This was Amstrad's series of machines. Amstrad was founded by British entrepreneur Alan Sugar, initially as a hi-fi company before breaking into the computer market with the successful CPC range. Their most successful model was the IBM-compatible PC 1512, which retailed at £399 and sold to homes as well as businesses. It

scooped 25 per cent of the European market in personal computers and had that innovative feature, the mouse.

Personal computer users have strong tribal loyalties to the Mac or PC. There may not be much substantive difference between the two systems, which are essentially trying to do the same thing. Macintosh software is typically favoured by users of graphical applications – its origins were in programs like MacPaint, which was so visual and so unusual for a computer when it was launched that it made instant converts. Because the one type of interface came, more or less, out of the same source of thinking as the other, some kind of dispute as to which was the true path and who had stolen whose ideas was inevitable. Apple Computer Inc. v. Microsoft Corporation was an attempt to prevent Microsoft using a GUI which looked like a Mac. In the middle

Amstrad computers, the brainchild of the British entrepreneur Lord Sugar, broke into the market due to their low price and their inclusion of a mouse.

The Sinclair Spectrum ZX80 brought the computing revolution to the masses. Significantly cheaper than its competitors, it made the computer an essential household item.

of it, Xerox sued Apple. Both cases were copyright-infringement claims. Both Apple and Xerox lost. But every computer owner knows whether a Mac or a PC is best.

Fun and games

Consumers have changed the way computers are used. People wanted to engage in games and that led to the success of personal computers. But this has not been the only influence of gaming on computing. The computer games industry has spawned a range of technical developments that would not otherwise have happened, since computer users from the 1950s onwards enjoyed their knowledge of the secret language of coding and their mastery of unwelcoming interfaces. Graphics, controllers, fantasy and exciting scenarios are all creatures of gaming, which has been driven by the twin needs of realism and release.

Computer games have a history of their own, but a few notable things can be highlighted.

- Pub and arcade machines are too limiting. More complex, extended-play games engage the player better, but require more computing power. Taking on the computer means that the program itself has to be smart and allow the game characters to behave in unexpected ways.

- Without good graphics and a good storyline, a game is valueless. The computing effort is directed towards speed and quality of display – different needs from the business computer user, but then feeding across into everyday computing as the achievements from the games industry are recognized.

- Solo-player games have long since been superseded by interactive play. To ensure gamers can take on remote, skilled opponents, games need to connect to the Internet and not be limited by available bandwidth.

- The lure of the sofa and television is not to be ignored. Consoles provide an ideal

Gaming has become a multibillion-dollar industry. The PlayStation 4 has impressive computing power and yet is solely dedicated to gaming and media playback.

way to play without having to sit up at a computer screen or go to the pub.

We all like our secret worlds. A console has only a handful of buttons and is less flexible than a computer keyboard. So, not to be out-done by coders, games have developed their own arcana: the meanings of the PlayStation symbols △, □, ○ and X might be imagined to be a secret code, but they are just the controls .

Mice in the PARC

People think of the Xerox Corporation as a company that made photocopiers. Indeed, Xerox thought of themselves this way and because of that self-perception they failed to exploit the best invention they may have had.

Xerox operated a research and development facility at Palo Alto, California, called the Palo Alto Research Center (Xerox PARC for short). Xerox PARC is where the original idea of using a mouse to move a pointer on the computer's screen and a click of a mouse-button to direct the computer was born. Controlling a computer using a pointer only makes sense if the information on the screen is presented in a two-dimensional, or graphical, way – a complete departure from the traditional sort of programming using lines of text.

Only Xerox was making its money – lots of it – from manufacturing and leasing copiers. During the computer revolution, photocopying began to give way to printing using devices directly connected to the computer, though subsequently offices centralized printing at 'multi-functional devices', which take care of both printing and (when needed) copying. Unfortunately for them, Xerox surrendered their brilliant idea of a mouse without so much as a squeak.

It wasn't just the user interface that was changing. The way computers stored data had also undergone another change. The old delay lines and CRT memory had long been extinct, replaced by magnetic storage, but even magnetic arrangements had evolved. Long spools of tape were slow – you have to reel through metres of it to get to the place you need – and two-dimensional arrays of magnetic storage were expensive. Still, early personal computers used nothing more complicated than an audio cassette machine for magnetic

PALO ALTO RESEARCH CENTER

XEROX

The mouse was developed at the headquarters of the Xerox corporation's research facility in Silicon Valley. But the company was so used to making copiers, they were unable to exploit their most original invention.

The floppy disk was the essential storage mechanism for early personal computers. It could hold programs and files by means of magnetic storage.

Electronic mail

It now seems outlandish that people used to communicate with their co-workers by writing them memos. Not only that, but bosses would dictate the memo to a secretary, who would write it down in shorthand and then transcribe it on a typewriter. (Shorthand gave way to dictating machines, to save secretarial time, but the good old memo persisted.)

Electronic mail changed all that. With computers in the office all being networked, it was possible to bypass the whole memo business and get an instant response. Sure, you could have done that by a phone-call, but sometimes the written form is better,

storage. But the magnetic 'floppy' disk – first 8-inch, then 5¼-inch and ultimately 3½-inch – came into being. These allowed for reliability, random-access and low cost. Only when cheap CD-ROM (and Blu-ray) alternatives and super-compact flash memory came on to the scene did magnetic storage for personal computers pass into history.

FLASH

The secret is in the silicon. The usual difficulty with memory on a silicon chip is that its content disappears when the power is switched off, but flash memory solves the problem, using a 'floating gate' that traps electrons in a sandwich layer within the semiconductor. When the voltage is switched off, the electrons don't escape unless an external power source interferes and changes the state of the gate. So now long-term memory has become miniaturized, just like circuits.

All splendid, but flash memory is not suitable for everything and questions have been asked about durability. Essentially the issue is how often you can rewrite flash memory. Where it's being used (as in your camera's memory card, or on your laptop's USB stick) for write-once, access-often applications, there's no problem. But industrial systems need to erase and write over old data and for these purposes reliability may be lower. I don't need to resave 10,000 times on the same stick, but a super-computer might do this every second. So mainframes tend not to rely on flash.

Longer-term memory can now be stored in 'flash', which is fast to access, but there is a weakness – information can only be written to it approximately 10,000 times before it will fail.

which is why we had memos in the first place. Like memos, email can be responded to when it's convenient. Initial efforts at email were bizarrely informal, as most bosses couldn't type, so uppercase letters were used rarely and grammatical rules only occasionally honoured in the earliest email. Sooner or later email became an external, as well as an internal, phenomenon. Faxes, letters and telexes – the external equivalent of memos – gave way to email as well, with a consequent improvement in spelling, presentation and grammar.

Sending email outside the company was considered very risky. These days we think of risks in terms of hacking and firewalls and security, but then it was all about knowing whether the message would arrive. The technical problem was finding the path through a communications network that

In 1969, a student at UCLA recorded the first message ever sent over ARPANET, which formed the basis of the modern Internet.

CUSTOMER SERVICE

might break down. Unlike a physical letter, which needs to keep intact along its journey, an electronic message is just a bunch of disembodied bits that can be broken into convenient parcels and – with suitable envelope information – reassembled at the receiving end. Breaking up a message facilitates sending it along the most efficient pathway, exploiting the idea that a network connects sender and receiver.

The Internet

Playing games on your home computer and being able to get some office work such as word processing done at home was all very well. But what made the personal computer an essential addition to every household was the Internet.

The origins of the Internet are intrinsically bound up with email and, as with so many things in the development of computing, the needs of the military authorities. The United States' Defense Advanced Research Projects Agency was founded in response to the launch of the Sputnik satellite in 1957 and was responsible for funding many transformative projects in a broad range of research areas. The research related to computing was chiefly carried on at household-name universities in the US, such as Harvard and MIT on the East Coast and Stanford, Berkeley and the University of California, Los Angeles (UCLA) on the West Coast. Other sites, such as Carnegie Mellon (in New York State) and the Universities of Illinois and Utah, were also involved. Communications between these various centres was difficult and, in 1966, thinking began on how they could be connected to bring the researchers

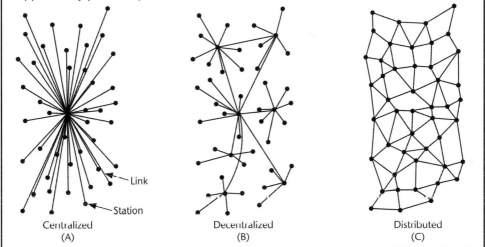

THE NETWORK IDEA

Paul Baran, working for the RAND Corporation, showed in 1968 that sending messages along a 'distributed' communications network would provide greater reliability if an outage were to happen at any particular point in the network.

Link
Station
Centralized
(A)

Decentralized
(B)

Distributed
(C)

'closer together' in a virtual sense. The idea of connecting them with a network and using packet-switching to improve reliability of communications was born.

Over time the network, called ARPANET, became less closely associated with ARPA's projects and grew into a more general communications medium for research institutions. There was an awkward relationship between telecommunications providers – without whom the network was nothing – and its users, particularly over who should control the protocols and standards for communications. Ultimately, by the time of the computer revolution, the Internet was a public communications medium.

But it was content as well as communications that made the Internet come of age. In 1991, inter-university communications included access to feed from a camera that showed the state of the coffee pot next to the Trojan Room in the Cambridge University computer lab. No doubt this was helpful to those saved a fruitless trip downstairs to find the pot empty; quite what use it was to people on another continent to know how fired up with caffeine the Cambridge researchers might be was another matter. But the live coffee-pot feed was an illustration of what you could do with the Internet: you could make available content, changing in real time, to viewers a long way away. Soon you could get a lot more than webcam coffee-pot data: the World Wide Web had been born.

In contrast to the 'Net', the origins of the Web are European, rather than American. There were two issues: on the

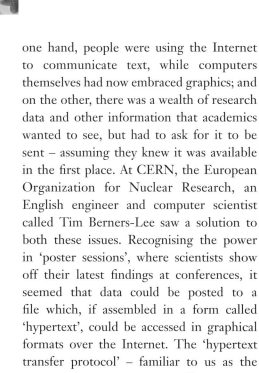

one hand, people were using the Internet to communicate text, while computers themselves had now embraced graphics; and on the other, there was a wealth of research data and other information that academics wanted to see, but had to ask for it to be sent – assuming they knew it was available in the first place. At CERN, the European Organization for Nuclear Research, an English engineer and computer scientist called Tim Berners-Lee saw a solution to both these issues. Recognising the power in 'poster sessions', where scientists show off their latest findings at conferences, it seemed that data could be posted to a file which, if assembled in a form called 'hypertext', could be accessed in graphical formats over the Internet. The 'hypertext transfer protocol' – familiar to us as the 'HTTP' prefix on web addresses – provided a technical solution to making content available to anyone who wanted access over the net.

CLOUD

Once upon a time, little diagrams explained to computer-users how to do new things like use the Internet. The little diagrams conventionally depicted the disembodied, distributed Internet service as a cloud. So, in a classic case of symbol turning into reality, the 'Cloud' is now where it is. And what is 'it'? Well, now, it's everything: not just where the content on the Internet comes from, but where your photos are stored, where your 'software-as-a-service' comes from and where the money is made in computing. It's big business, too: huge special-purpose data facilities are operated by companies like Amazon and Google, where giant servers provide the electronic guts of storage. It's a bit uglier than the cloud drawing, but in terms of convenience, if anything can be accessed or provided remotely, it's heavenly.

Tim Berners-Lee, a computer scientist at CERN, took inspiration from 'poster sessions' at universities in designing hypertext, which made it possible to access everything on the internet.

The idea caught on immediately. CERN's web software was released in 1991; web browsers became publicly available in late 1993; the growth in web servers was exponential; and soon every business, every governmental organization – and even every family – seemed to want to have its own website; e-commerce was born.

Dot.com doom

And with it came a rush of new businesses to market, eager to find capital to grow its proposal. The investors piled in: e-commerce was the future. Anything with 'dot com' in its name was a stock to pick. Companies that had never made a cent of profit were achieving stock-market listings and raising capital on the strength of nothing more solid than an optimistic business plan. It should have been obvious that this was another stock market bubble. Some failed, many merged, lots of money was lost, corporate finance advisers were fined for misleading investors and then the devastation of the '9/11' terrorist attack on the World Trade Centre in New York City in 2001 triggered a stock market downturn in 2002.

The dot.com boom and bust did not mean there was anything intrinsically wrong with the Internet. Some of the Internet's features, though, have disrupted traditional businesses:

- Content is very often free. This is a direct consequence of the open, academic, sharing-of-data culture derived from the web's inventors and first users. Free content means that things that once were paid for (newspapers in particular) are perceived to be under threat. It also means that content-providers have recourse to advertising – frequently smart advertising informed by machine learning algorithms – to fund their operations.
- Shopping can now be done at home, since there is better choice and ease of comparison. Much has been written about the impact on traditional patterns of retail distribution and the demise of town centres (though people still seem to go to the shops and eating out has attractions that could never be replaced by a home-delivery service). It also means that logistics and packaging companies have thrived.
- Without telecommunications providers, the Internet is nothing. There is a strange symbiosis: the telecommunications industry derives large revenues from users who are not making phone calls or sending texts (or, in times past, faxes) but doing computing. Computing without telecommunications would rarely be more than old-style calculation and office work. At the same time, there is a difference: a telecommunications business thrives as more users join it (what the economists call a network effect) – thus tending towards a single provider who dominates the marketplace and requiring the intervention of a regulator and the constraints of competition policy; whereas the Internet is open and largely unregulated.

With email and the Internet, computing became information and communications technology (ICT) in which 'computing' seems to have taken a subordinate role. ICT is embedded in everything; seemingly every piece of electrical machinery contains some information and communication device. Increasingly, computing devices embedded in everyday objects will be able to send and receive data and also connect with each other via the Internet. This interconnection of everyday objects is called 'the Internet of things'. The effect this will have on society is much debated.

Things are only connected to the Internet because they contain embedded computers. Computers have been inside objects for a long time – they are there because machines need to be controlled and control is most adaptable when it is done by a computer. So miniaturization and the creation of microprocessors had a useful

INTERNET OF THINGS

There has been hype: 'The Internet of things has the potential to have a greater impact on society than the first digital revolution,' according to Sir Mark Walport, the UK Government's Chief Scientific Adviser. There has been more hype: 'Cities will have countless autonomous, intelligently functioning IT systems that will have perfect knowledge of users' habits,' according to the engineering firm Siemens. There have been scare-stories: 'So your car becomes a network computer, and the vulnerability there is that if I can hack into it [the onboard computer], I can take over your car. This is not hypothetical,' says one expert, citing a case where researchers hacked a Jeep's braking and transmission system. There has also been the reality: a smart meter in your home that learns to adjust when the heating and hot water come on, and allows you to change the settings from your phone. In the UK, there is a type of smart thermostat called Nest: 'Since October 2011, Nesters have saved 12,042,986,211 kWh. That's enough energy to pop all the popcorn needed to fill 418,000 cinemas.'

The Internet of things refers to the many devices that now have computers and network connectivity embedded in them. The Internet used to be only accessed by computers, but now is used in goods as varied as watches and fridges.

side effect: it meant that computers could be installed, silently and invisibly, inside any electrical object. Cameras, printers, cars, washing machines, game consoles and thermostats are all much more than their non-electronic forebears had been. With computing power and a connection to the Internet, the status and control information that the machines spin out can go off into the ether and contribute to the vast bank of data about how we live and work.

Laptop

Nowhere is the shift from old-fashioned 'computing' – in the sense of number-crunching of arithmetical calculations – to

The 2005 Toyota Camry suffered from stack overflow. Stack overflow is a condition of computers when they attempt to use more space than is available. In the case of the Camry, this affected the computer-controlled throttle system, causing the car to accelerate despite the attempts of its driver to control the vehicle. The car came flying off the highway in Oklahoma, killing one person and injuring another. The driver probably didn't even know that there was a computer regulating the accelerator. The result? The court held the car manufacturers liable, awarding $3 million in damages and triggering an investigation into how basic computer system design errors had crept into what ought to have been a simple enhancement to the car.

these characteristics, it sold well – and that encouraged the major manufacturers to put significant effort into the design of lightweight, large-screen portable machines.

The laptop as we know it came out of this frenzy of development. The GRiD Compass computer had two innovations that have stuck: the flat screen and the idea that the screen folds down on to the keyboard in what is called a 'clamshell' design. Laptops can be slotted into a briefcase and provide access to data and a full range of functionality without being tied to a single location.

More and more computing power crammed into smaller and smaller spaces has enabled laptops to compete with chunkier desktop personal computers – so, one might ask, why do people have a desktop computer at all? The answer is probably to do with size of the display, but also to do with communications: a full-function modern

information and communications more evident than in the miniaturization of computers for use by individuals. Hand-in-hand with the computing revolution came the reduction in size of personal computers, beginning with the laptop.

The notion of a portable terminal, which executives could use while on the move, emerged in the 1970s. An early example of a completely independent, portable computer was the Osborne 1, released in 1981. It looked like a suitcase, it weighed as much as a suitcase (13kg/29lb), its top opened up to form a fold-down keyboard and its monochrome screen was so tiny (13cm/5 ⅝in) as to be almost invisible in the middle of the machine. Despite all

The Osborne 1 was the first portable computer, weighing a hefty 13kg (29lb).

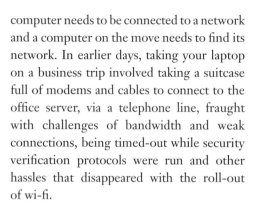

computer needs to be connected to a network and a computer on the move needs to find its network. In earlier days, taking your laptop on a business trip involved taking a suitcase full of modems and cables to connect to the office server, via a telephone line, fraught with challenges of bandwidth and weak connections, being timed-out while security verification protocols were run and other hassles that disappeared with the roll-out of wi-fi.

Miniaturization means that even the computers in our phones are as powerful as desktops of just a few years prior.

WATCH THIS SPACE

In 2010 one might have been tempted to think that miniaturization of personal computing devices had reached a point from which only a return was possible, as mobile phones started getting larger again in order to accommodate better graphics, more detailed apps, more legibility for emails and so forth. Some phones are shrunk-down tablet computers. Despite that change, a new generation of miniature devices appeared: watches that link to phones but provide more services than simply telling the time are the most obvious and probably the most popular. Other things are out there too, with clothing, spectacles, jewellery and headphones all appearing in headlines as the latest thing. Your guess about what will catch on is probably better than mine. Smart prostheses seem to have a future; and then there is the nanobot – the computerized micro-machine that is so small that it roams around inside your body, carrying out construction or destruction processes that your own repair and immune systems cannot manage for themselves.

The trend towards miniaturization of computing devices continued unabated after the development of laptops. The next stage was the creation of 'personal digital assistants' (PDAs), with rather limited power and functionality, whose chief contribution to progress was to allow business folk to stay connected to their email 24 hours a day. Then, in another marriage with consumer electronics, Apple combined into a single box their best-selling iPod, a music storage and playback device, with a mobile phone, email and other applications to create the iPhone. This has been extensively developed and mimicked and raises rather philosophical questions about whether it is a computer and whether it has changed the definition of computing to fit the uses that people find for the device. In thinking about miniaturization it is thus tempting to see an evolution towards tiny devices, such as nanobots and wearable computers.

Nixing nanotrends

In all this rush to embrace the kind of machines that do not embarrass teenagers, modern, but still traditional, forms of computing machinery might be forgotten. Yet they persist. To begin with, even desktop 'personal computers' tend to be linked by a local network: in offices and schools, the user's machine is a 'client' whose real computing power resides on one or more servers that may be located some distance from the apparently self-contained desktop machine. The organizational structure is suspiciously similar to the old mainframe-and-terminal model that was supposed to have been supplanted by go-ahead executives carrying their entire global business on a laptop. Indeed, the mainframe itself is by no means dead: it may be unobtrusive, but it's still there and it is ever more powerful.

MODERN MAINFRAME

While businesses have continued to use mainframe computers throughout the period of the computing revolution, another breed of computer emerged at the other end of the size spectrum – the supercomputer. Mainframes and super-computers can be distinguished :

Mainframe	Supercomputer
Looks Bauhaus, Mies van der Rohe sober	Looks Montréal Palais des Congrès, wow-factor
Speed in MIPS (millions of instruction per second)	Speed in Petaflops ($\times 10^{15}$ floating-point operations per second)
Lots of concurrent transactions initiated by multiple users	Enormous computations by one-at-a-time users
Shaped by input-output demands of users	Shaped by large datasets and speed requirement
Business users	Academic and military users

Each year a 'TOP500' list of monster supercomputers is published. Some notable contenders slugging it out for the big computer championship have included:

- Flyweight (1976): Cray-1, a specially designed machine installed at the Los Alamos National Laboratory. It weighed in at 160 megaflops; the Cray computer company designed it with especially short wires to keep it speedy for its scientific (and classified military) applications.
- Welterweight (2008): Black Widow, a 100 gigaflop machine built for the US National Security Agency (NSA). Its purpose was to check on email and phone call traffic and pre-identify terrorist and other security threats.
- Heavyweight (2017): Cheyenne 5.3 petaflop machine used by the American National Center for Atmospheric Research. It looks out for high-impact weather.
- Off the scale (2013): Milky-way 2, a 33.9 petaflop machine in Guangzhou, China, developed by the Chinese National University of Defense Technology. It's used for 'government security operations'.

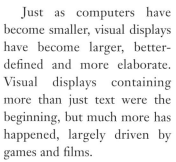

Just as computers have become smaller, visual displays have become larger, better-defined and more elaborate. Visual displays containing more than just text were the beginning, but much more has happened, largely driven by games and films.

• The earliest graphic displays – such as an IBM 2250 system from the 1960s – allowed the user to control the display with a 'light pen'. The device picked up on the moment the beam of electrons travelled across the computer screen, thereby

Early graphic displays used 'light pens' to interact with the screen.

UTAH TEAPOT

An icon of graphic design is the Utah teapot. In 1975, graphics designer Martin Newell, working at the University of Utah, used a Melitta teapot as a case study for modelling its surface, describing its geometry and making the data available publicly. The teapot thus became commonly used as a reference object for graphics work.

The teapot is not, however, exactly what it seems. The usual rendering of the teapot makes it flatter and more squashed-out than the Melitta original. Various explanations have been given for this, ranging from the shape of pixels to 'we liked it better'. But if you prefer, you can still buy a teapot of the original, uncomputerized shape, as they are still being manufactured in Germany.

Martin Newell attempted to digitally re-create the Melitta teapot in 1975 and it has since been used as an important reference point for computer graphics.

Computers have greatly aided design work with the use of specialized programs, whether in architecture, aerospace engineering or even the creation of prosthetics.

identifying the location of the pen. Cleverer graphics required the image to be manipulated and redesigned.

- Rendering a three-dimensional object on to two-dimensional space requires the object to be atomized into 'primitives' – typically little triangles, each of which represents a piece of the object's surface. The primitives can include the invisible parts – surfaces that are hidden because they are on its far side. Then the object can be moved around, as the triangles are reconfigured by the computer model.

- Computer-aided design is thus not about using the computer screen as an alternative drawing board, but about the quality of the model that the computer uses to assist the designer.

- Graphics quality needs more than the ability to turn 3-D objects around on a 2-D screen. There are the challenges of perspective, shading, texture, animation and pixellation. Pixels are responsible for the annoying staircase appearance of diagonal or curved lines blown up to large scale. Whereas design drawings need different standards, graphics in games and films aim for photo-realism.

- Graphics can also be generated by programs, enabling scenery or characters to be inserted into regular movie footage and facilitating the development of virtual reality environments. Games are at the forefront of graphics developments, but non-leisure simulations such as flight-deck trainers need good graphics to be truly effective.

Whether it's a games console, a mainframe, a smartphone, a laptop or a four-function electronic calculator, one thing characterizes all such computing machinery: their dependency on humans for mobility and connectedness. The computer revolution has now given rise to the communications revolution. Information is everywhere and everyone can comment on it – and does. But can you trust the information you find? And how safe is it anyway?

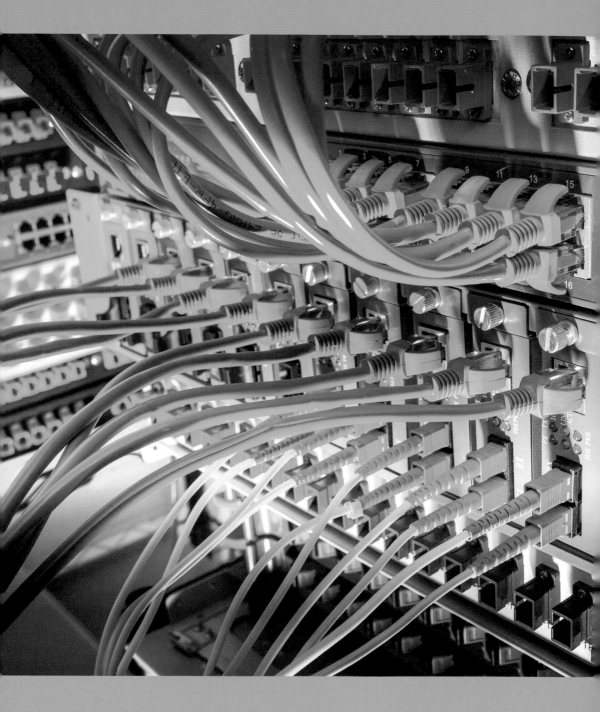

Chapter 8

THE WAY WE LIVE NOW

With the merger of computing into communications, social media developed. Increased use of the Internet for commerce as well as sharing of information has allowed big data and its exploitation to emerge, raising difficult social questions about privacy and control. Encryption, firewalls, hacking and cyber-attacks have all become part of our daily concerns and data science has become an academic discipline.

The world has become a deeply interconnected place thanks to the fibre optic cables that carry the Internet to homes and businesses everywhere.

We are connected. We always have been, in the marketplace, in the pub, at the football match. We became connected remotely through the postal system, the telegraph, the phone and now the computer, which during the revolution evolved into a species of communications technology. The computer spawned new types of network.

While we have seen how email and the Internet depend on a communications network for their resilience and pervasiveness, it was not self-evident that the communications power of computing would lead to new types of social interaction. Network effects are observed when the more participants there are, the more important it becomes for everyone else to participate. This is the characteristic that makes the marketplace work and that makes going to a football game better than watching it at home. But it needs a nucleus, something that makes the core group hang together and create the essential desirability of belonging: a community of interest.

Social media like Facebook, Twitter and Instagram have changed the way we interact with each other.

@

Back in the day, if you wanted to order 11 fancy waistcoats at six guineas each, you could find on your invoice the statement '11 waistcoats @ 6 gns' and everyone would know what was meant. So, typewriter keyboards, designed for commercial use, had a convenient @ key, to avoid typing '(a)' or even the word 'at'.

Computer scientist Ray Tomlinson, of BBN Technologies, in Cambridge, Massachusetts, was working on the Arpanet – the forerunner of the internet – in 1971. He looked for a symbol on his computer keyboard that he could use in the address code to separate the target computer from the individual the message was aimed at. He chose '@' because it made sense in context, and was otherwise rarely used.

Information society

The ease of communication that the computing revolution brought about provided fertile ground in which new networks could be tested. The structures and models are diverse, but some have prospered where others have barely survived – or not. Some are specialist forums for members with a shared technical interest, seeking help and disseminating tips. Some are chatrooms that might be viewed as a form of virtual marketplace. But the super-successes of the present century are not like that; their attractiveness is remarkable and their business model is different.

• Facebook started in 2004 as a directory for Harvard students containing photos and basic information. Its launch was overwhelming – everybody wanted to register. Within a month it had opened to other Ivy League schools. By 2005 there were 2,000 colleges and 25,000 high schools participating. The secret? Everyone wants to share and it gave you the chance to pass judgment ('like'). Facebook is a push system: in the same way that early adopters of the World Wide Web wanted their own website, Facebook allows its users to post updates about themselves and their community and this information is fascinating enough to the friends of those users to make it worthwhile.

• Twitter started in 2006 as a way to reduce the cost of sending texts (SMS messages). Its exponential growth can be traced back to a tech conference in 2007 where tweets were publicly displayed and all the delegates wanted to participate. The limit – 140 characters (related to its

LEADER OF THE FREE WORLD

All the pollsters knew that Adlai Stevenson was going to win the 1952 US presidential election. Then along came UNIVAC, one of those monstrous electronic brains of the era, and said otherwise. A new program was run on the machine that compared the 1952 returns with previous election data and it did it fast. UNIVAC said that Eisenhower would garner 438 votes in the electoral college, against 266 needed to win. The broadcaster CBS knew that this had to be tosh, so didn't use the information in its broadcasts. Later that same night, the electoral college votes came in and Eisenhower had 442. UNIVAC had won and the broadcaster had lost a scoop.

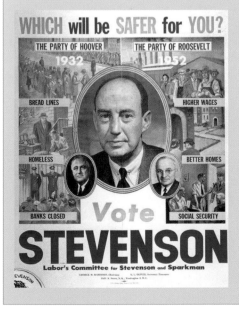

Fast forward to the 21st century. New times, new technologies. In 2000, Democratic candidate Al Gore claimed to have been instrumental in creating the Internet; he lost on electoral college votes. In 2008 the power of technology was used, rather than alluded to. Barack Obama's election team used machine learning to target voters and ensure the right messages were heard by the target groups. Obama won.

Computers have played a role in politics for decades. The UNIVAC accurately predicted Dwight Eisenhower's presidential victory against the odds.

Twitter began as a way of sending free texts, but its unique features, including the 140 character limit and its hashtags, have propelled it to great heights.

TWITTER, TWEET. RETWEET and the Twitter logo are trademarks of Twitter, Inc or its affiliates.

origins in texting) – and the user-driven abilities to identify yourself with an @ symbol, use hashtags for links and retweet cool stuff were all important to its success. Like Facebook, it's a push system; but it's used for news and opinions and so appeals to a different community.

Social media works best in partnership with mobile phone technology. The iPhone was launched in 2007 and the simultaneous success of social media apps with smartphones is no coincidence. Facebook and Twitter are for people on the go, with cameras built into their phones, with communications rather than computations at the forefront of their mind. It's all about staying in touch.

Content is free

Today, content is rarely charged for. People volunteer their material; in a way, it doesn't matter whether its quality is high. The results, which people can find irritating, can be criticized as trivia, as post-truth, as unbalanced or offensive. More

The free online encyclopedia Wikipedia is a vast depository of human knowledge that eclipses all print media.

substantial fears about free content concern the slow demise of paid-for content, a topic usually discussed under the rubric 'the future of print journalism'. On the other hand, the network idea has allowed a free-content information source to grow, again to the exclusion of traditional print media: the online encyclopaedia.

Wikipedia started in 2001. It claims (for Wikipedia is the fullest, if not necessarily the most unbiased, source of information about itself) to have over 5 million articles, the equivalent of 2,500 volumes of *Encyclopedia Britannica*. (My ageing print edition of the *Britannica*, complete with faux-leather bindings, has 30 volumes, two volumes of index and something called a 'propaedia', which is a sort of user's guide.) Wikipedia's content is provided, improved and moderated by its unpaid users. Unlike social media, it's less push than pull: you go to Wikipedia for information, then you're drawn into its community and tempted to contribute. And you don't tend to use it on your phone: it's for looking things up, when sitting at your desk. Yet another difference is that Wikipedia is a not-for-profit undertaking.

The print version of the Encyclopedia Britannica *has been almost made redundant due to the availability of free content on the Internet from sites like Wikipedia.*

These huge systems – some popstars have over 100 million followers on Twitter; over 50 billion photos have been uploaded to Facebook – consume vast computing resources. This all has to be financed somehow, since a paid-for network does not expand virally like these have. Advertising, though not the only source of revenue, is a vital component of success. Facebook has 3 million advertisers. Another source of revenue is data licensing. The way we live now is all about data, since even the advertising is valueless unless it is suitably targeted.

So it is no surprise that machine learning drives the businesses of the online giants, from social media companies to Google and Amazon. What is, possibly, more of a surprise is the lack of consensus on the question

Online companies like Amazon jealously wield the data they receive from visitors to their sites to enhance their profits.

of privacy. Everything posted, everything searched for, every single transaction carried out online creates a trail of content and metadata, which is there for the giants to use.

Big world, small data

The data is big. Actually, what this means is that the data is small, some of it very small indeed, but that there is a great deal of it. With more tiny pieces of data being generated by your phone wherever you go, whatever you do, and by whatever equipment you use, the volume of data is overwhelming. Apparently it's measured in zettabytes – trillions of gigabytes. And that is a powerful source of intelligence, if you know how to mine it and how to exploit it.

SIXTA

April 1940. German wireless activity in the Baltic was different from usual. Something must be up. A young recruit to Bletchley Park phoned the Admiralty on a special telephone line. Well, frankly, it took a bit more than some upstart burbling about beeps in the ether to convince a commander, a captain and a rear admiral, who collectively had many decades of sea-years' experience, that an invasion was about to take place. But it was. Bletchley Park was doing more than code-breaking: it was looking at the signals themselves, and from the pattern of signals they believed that an invasion of Norway was about to take place. The warning was ignored, but the signals interpreters at Bletchley were right. Even admirals have to learn the hard way sometimes.

Before, during and after they managed to break the Enigma cipher at Bletchley Park, there was metadata analysis. In due course it was organized into something called 'Sixta', standing for Hut 6 Traffic Analysis. Sixta's analysis of directions, call signs, frequencies and volumes told the signals intelligence officers things regardless of whether the codebreakers were able to figure out the content of messages.

Seventy years on, pattern, packet and metadata analysis and their information continue to play a role at GCHQ, Bletchley Park's successor, in assessing communications relevant to national security. The relationship between secrecy and computing has ever been a close one.

Hut 6 at Bletchley Park was where traffic analysis took place. A similar process takes place assessing metadata today at GCHQ.

Exploitation sounds improper; yet we don't really know what is private and what is not. The signals are confused. In EU law, the General Data Protection Regulation gives citizens a 'right to be forgotten' – which means that personal data held by another person must be erased in some circumstances. But the circumstances are rather limited and if the 'data subject' has consented to the processing of their data it's going to be hard to be forgotten. Social media sites and essentially everyone else with a commercial interest will almost invariably ask for consent to process your data for any and every imaginable purpose. This doesn't trouble us, except when something happens and then it may be too late.

Perhaps we need to be more careful: certainly we are urged to do so. Seemingly every time we sign up for anything we have to create a password. Even in the workplace every system has a different password. It has got so out of hand that the head of the National Cyber Security Centre – part of GCHQ – said in 2017 that demands for regularly changing long passwords comprising numbers, funny characters, upper- and lowercase letters and what have you means that people are asked to memorize 600 new digits for passwords every month. Then he said it was completely pointless and damaging to security, because people share, write them down and adopt other practices to keep on top of all this nonsense.

So you might now be asking why we have to have all these passwords in the first place. The main reason is authentication:

PROFUMO

The conflict between concerns of privacy, scrutiny and security can be illustrated with a few historical examples.

- 1586. Anthony Babington did not want anyone reading his letters, because they gave details of a plan to free Mary Queen of Scots, at the time held as a political prisoner by the government of Queen Elizabeth of England. So he used a cipher – which was broken by a very early predecessor of GCHQ.

- 1961. John Profumo was the Secretary of State for War. His resignation was the result of a press campaign investigating his relationship with a 19-year-old model who was allegedly involved with the Soviet naval attaché as well. Profumo denied any impropriety, but he was caught in a lie to Parliament and he had to go. The heady mix of spying, lying, high society and low life was nectar for journalists, putting him in the very centre of the conflicts between public office, privacy and publicity.

Duncan Campbell wished to present a television documentary on the launch of Zircon but found himself at odds with the British government. The broader debate over privacy, security and the public's right to know continues today.

- 1987. Duncan Campbell, an investigative journalist, had a scoop. The British Government was going to launch Zircon, a signals intelligence satellite. The government wanted to ban the planned television documentary that would spill the beans, but then the news story became one about the public's right to know and whether banning could prevent MPs from viewing the programme.

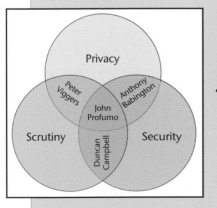

- 2009. Sir Peter Viggers, the Hon. Member for Gosport, found himself the object of ridicule when it turned out that the 'expenses' incurred in representing his constituents included the sum of £1,600 spent on a floating duck house. The MP almost certainly had no idea that his expenses claims would be scrutinized by anyone other than the person who paid them.

One solution to the security dilemma is two-factor authentication. This requires a passcode sent to one device to be input into another.

cyberattacks are happening all the time, for a variety of reasons; and then we are daft enough to fall for ploys that get us to give away our secrets without the need for an attack on a firewall at all.

Getting around, under or over the firewall has as much ingenuity in it as scaling, undermining and blagging your way into a walled city during a mediaeval siege.

- The old-fashioned hacker tries various ways to get in. Stealing the key, assuming that the password is 'password' or '12345678' and other password-based attacks are attempts to batter in the front gate.
- There is the even older method of the Trojan horse – something that looks rather interesting and so is allowed in, only to

in the bad old days, before computing became communications technology, we authenticated ourselves by facial and vocal recognition, or by a signature if communicating in writing. With remote, real-time online communication, the old methods have not (at least for the first 20 years of what used to be called the 'information society') been feasible. In many instances, complex passwords were the answer. But the NCSC says there are better ways to authenticate.

The accepted standard is two-factor (or multi-factor) authentication: something the user possesses, plus something the user knows (like a card plus PIN). There are various ways of doing this: nowadays the civil service will typically send you a text message to your phone (something you own) with a code-number, after you have presented yourself with your username and password (something you know).

The danger of cyberattacks has never been more real. The Wannacry attack in May 2017 briefly crippled the NHS in the UK, FedEx and Deutsche Bahn, among other companies.

Firewall

So that makes us all free from cyberattack and other ways of undermining our computing security? Alas, no. First of all,

show its true self later. The malware that allowed $100 million to be siphoned out of the Bangladesh Central Bank in 2016 was probably introduced as a macro embedded in a Microsoft Word document, sent in as an attachment. But there may have been someone on the inside, too – another well-trusted method to help besiegers.

- Ways in include backdoors and 'zero-day' defects in the system – backdoors are apertures deliberately left by the designers; zero-day attacks are based on weaknesses the designers do not know about until day zero (which is typically the day their problems begin).
- Phishing attacks depend on the innocence, or if you prefer, the stupidity, of the victim. The besieger doesn't need to

fuss about the firewall if the insider can be duped into passing on the details he wants. Most people are savvy enough to know that the email telling them they won the Ruritanian lottery is unlikely to be real, but imitation websites posing as the real thing and imitation emails that look authentic enough to have come from your real bank can deceive people into logging on, putting in details and regretting it all later.

- Another way is to overwhelm the defences of the defender by quasi-legitimate knocks on the door. Every business needs to deal with its customers and suppliers and making a convenient channel for them to communicate is essential – until the system is hijacked by a deluge of fake

CALIFORNIA LICENSE PLATE 35KGD203

The case was called 'In the Matter of the Search of an Apple iPhone Seized During the Execution of a Search Warrant on a Black Lexus IS300, California License Plate 35KGD203'. For something that raised one of the most difficult private-versus-public debates, it's a pretty indigestible name.

It was all about the FBI and an iPhone: after 10 failed password entry attempts, all data on the phone would be wiped. And the FBI wanted to get into the phone, because it belonged to one of the perpetrators of the San Bernardino shootings of December 2015, when 14 people were killed and 22 others injured in what was then the most serious terrorist incident since 9/11. Apple, the makers of the phone, were asked to create a backdoor that would bypass the phone's security and reveal the secrets of the killers. Apple said no. Chief executive Tim Cook said: 'We oppose this order, which has implications far beyond the legal case at hand. This moment calls for public discussion.'

The public discussion did not take place in the courtroom. The FBI withdrew from the case, when a hacker they had engaged found them a backdoor without needing the co-operation of Apple.

Tim Cook resisted the FBI's demands to provide a backdoor into the iPhone.

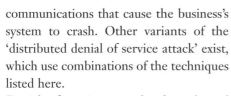
communications that cause the business's system to crash. Other variants of the 'distributed denial of service attack' exist, which use combinations of the techniques listed here.

- Denial of service can also be achieved through ransomware, which requires the victim to pay up in order to restore normal operations. An unhappy example of this kind of attack occurred in May 2017, when various hospitals and other service providers in the UK and elsewhere found themselves facing a computer screen saying, 'Oops, your files have been encrypted!'

The motives for getting in are not always for personal gain. 'Hacktivists' are people who hack into computers in order to expose or punish the organization whose site or system is under attack, for political reasons, for military reasons, or even just for a laugh.

Sign of the times

Now take signatures. You need to sign documents – but why? Usually it's because the other person with whom you are doing business needs to be able to confirm that it really was you who agreed to it, which then makes it hard for you to wriggle out of your contract. In days of instant commerce where signatories can be continents apart, this is clumsy and unreliable and the practice of having signatures 'witnessed' to prove that the person who is alleged to have signed did indeed sign looks quaint and mediaeval. So 'electronic signatures' were invented, which are possibly the most confusing things ever to have made their way into the world of computing.

- In 1999 the EU made a brave foray into the ultra-modern, with some legislation to facilitate e-signatures. Their definition is a joyous example of legal drafting:

GUY FAWKES

Hacktivists tend to favour weird and wonderful ways of describing themselves (Cult of the Dead Cow, LulzSec and PhineasFisher); the point being that anonymity is vital. Exposing secrets (official or commercial) is often illegal; undermining firewalls is illegal; and long sentences are handed down to cyber-exposers. Used in the film *V for Vendetta* (2005), in which an anarchist freedom fighter called 'V' wears a stylized Guy Fawkes mask, the mask has been adopted by hacktivists and become a symbol of wider popular protest.

The hacker group Anonymous has adopted the stylized Guy Fawkes mask as part of its uniform.

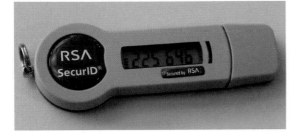

RSA tokens generate a digital 'key' to verify someone's identity.

'"Electronic signature" means data in electronic form that are attached to or logically associated with other electronic data and which serve as a method of authentication.' So, if that doesn't make you any wiser, let's try again.

- Some e-signing services allow authorized signatories to upload their signatures – yes, real signatures – and sign things on the go by tapping on their mobile devices, having signed in securely to the service, presumably using a password or two-factor authentication. Fair enough, but why the old-fashioned signature is still there is difficult to understand. It's probably the comfort factor: the logic that says keeping banknotes under the mattress is reassuring.

- You can go the whole hog and make it totally electronic, not that this has ever caught on for everyday documents. These fully digital methods produce a 'signature' that no human would recognize as such – a digital signature is a string of bits produced by cryptography. A familiar device is the 'RSA token', which generates a signature 'key' – but these devices were normally used to open online gateways, not to sign documents.

Once again the world of computing has become tangled up with encryption. Authentication is one application, but keeping communications confidential is another contemporary concern. It's been an issue in computing since we started using modern communications technology – in other words, since the invention of radio-telegraphy at the start of the 20th century.

Nowadays we are obsessed with secrecy, when we feel like it. Except when I post my entire life story on Facebook, I want everything to be secure from prying eyes. The idea of 'snoopers' peering at my emails is offensive, so I want to communicate in cipher. Sometimes, though, encrypting things that are not secrets can have the exact opposite effect to what was intended. So we should probably ask ourselves more often why things need to be a secret. This is true in the commercial world as well as in our private dealings.

Data and science

Not only do we succumb to the temptation to keep too much a secret, but we keep too much of everything. According to one source, in 2017 there were 400,000 tweets, 3.3 million Facebook posts and 500 hours of video uploaded to YouTube – and all this happens every 60 seconds. That's an awful lot of e-junk floating around in virtual space. Most of it will never be accessed again; and even stuff that is looked at this week will be forgotten by next month. We just have too much. The fear that we needed to keep things, just in case, has been turned into the problem of managing too much, not being able to find what we do need and selectivity. Businesses that once sent their paper files to 'storage' – a mysterious place where the papers would slowly decay into rat-fodder – now have electronic data-

8,616,460,799

What's in a number? In 1873 W.S. Jevons bet the world that nobody could factorize 8,616,460,799. Well, they could: it was certainly done by 1903 (the answer is 96,079 × 89,681, both of which are prime numbers). Jevons's point was a bit more significant than a maths test, though. It's a classic case of an NP problem (see page 63) that's hard to solve but easy to verify: once you know the factors, you can check the answer, but it's a monstrous task to search through the candidates to find the right one.

In 1976, Whitfield Diffie and Martin Hellman showed that you could have a practically unbreakable cipher using a 'public key' and a 'private key'. If I want you to communicate securely to me, I tell you my public key and you go off and encipher the message with the public key. It doesn't matter that someone eavesdropped on your message to me, because it's enciphered – and it doesn't matter that someone eavesdropped on my message sending out the public key either. This is because you can't, practically, compute the deciphering key – the private key – from the public one. Only I have the private key and, using

Martin Hellman and Whitfield Diffie established the idea of public key encryption.

it, I can peel off the encipherment and reveal what you were telling me. What this process needs is a 'trap door function' (easy to go one way, much harder to go back) for creating logically linked public and private keys.

The year after Diffie and Hellman published their paper, a practical trap door function was proposed in the form of the Rivest-Shamir-Adelman algorithm. The RSA trap door function was a rerun of Jevons's challenge. The public key would use a non-secret number that is the product of two primes, but only the holder of the private key would know what those two primes are.

The security of RSA depends on the Jevons principle that factorization of multi-digit numbers is just too hard: nobody yet has come up with an algorithm for factorization that can be done in polynomial time when the prime numbers are big enough – unless you happen to be using a thing called a quantum computer and even GCHQ hasn't (so far as we know) got one of those yet. It's a challenge in practical P-versus-NP computability. But once the computing power becomes available to bust the problem, the secrets of the world will lie wide open. My bank balance, for example: but it's not a secret that it's less than 8,616,460,799.

destruction policies to replace their old record-keeping policies.

Wherever there is a problem, there is a professor. Data science began in the 21st century and already has its own academic journals, dozens of British universities offering Masters' degrees and a prediction that in the US alone there will be 2.7

million jobs for data professionals by 2020.

In sum, data are big, networked and public. It is right that we have professors studying how we use this data and what it's all going to mean. Data are not 'ICT' because data is not the same as information and their creator may never expect them to be communicated. Data are, however, computing. Without data we have nothing to compute and without people there are no data.

SILICON VALLEY

Silicon Valley is the area near San Jose, CA that stretches around San Francisco Bay. It is the home to dozens of tech companies. In 1971 the concentration of industry and talent led a journalist to coin the phrase 'Silicon Valley' in a series of articles in *Electronic News*, because at that time the focus was on the industrial processes needed to purify silicon and manufacture semiconductor chips.

Since 1971 all sorts of places have become siliconized. Silicon Glen, in Scotland, enjoyed a decade or so in the limelight, before the tech companies that had settled there began to downsize or move away. Silicon Fen, near Cambridge, is the home of tech start-ups. Silicon Roundabout, in London, is a similar concept. Then, in the USA, there is the Silicon Prairie, near Dallas, or maybe the term refers to a belt of tech companies between Kansas City, KS, Des Moines, IA and Omaha, NB.

Silicon geographies have also been adopted in various parts of Europe, the Americas, Australia and Asia.

Everyone wants chips, it seems; but the point is surely that the computing industry, from chip manufacturers to data warehouses, is growing, everywhere.

Silicon Valley, the southern section of the San Francisco Bay area, is home to a vast number of technology firms. Its success has been reflected in the names given to the Silicon Prairie of Dallas, the Silicon Fen of Cambridge, UK and a variety of other places.

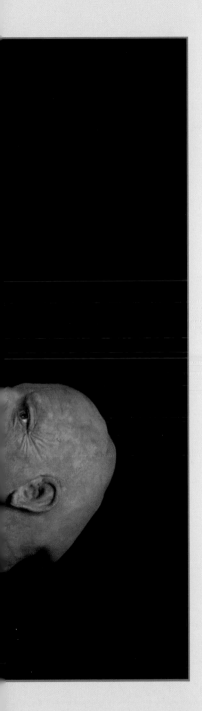

Chapter 9

COMPUTING FOR LIFE

The big question raised by the
appearance of fast, multi-purpose
electronic computers in the post-war
period was whether machines can
'think'. Fierce debate on the issue grew
into work on whether machines could
learn and adapt, leading to the first
steps in creating artificial intelligence
(AI). Early steps in AI included chess-
playing algorithms, optical recognition
and natural language processing. But
progress in this field has been slow.

*Can machines think? Since Alan Turing first
posed the Turing Test, researchers have pursued
the dream of artificial intelligence.*

Alan Turing's frustration with the National Physical Laboratory (NPL) was not solely down to the snail's pace at which his design for a computing machine was being realized. After designing the computer, he had spent months creating routines and programs for the machine, even though it was still a machine only on paper. When that had become increasingly pointless, he had turned his mind to the wider capabilities of computing machinery. For the Executive Committee of the NPL, computing machinery was to do calculations – that is to say, to solve mathematical equations, with numerical input and numerical output. Those who had seen what computing machinery could do in other practical contexts knew no such bounds, but were at risk of being thought fantastical.

Alan Turing and David Champernowne created a chess-playing algorithm called TuroChamp. The chess moves had to be worked out with pen and paper, but the principles were the same as those used by computerized chess programs.

A foretaste of what is to come

At Bletchley Park there had been extra-curricular discussions among the mathematicians and machine experts about the possibility of instructing a machine to play a game of chess. For a time, this seemed to be the epitome of computing power and a good deal of effort went into creating chess-playing algorithms. Some of these came into being, though not in the form of computer programs; instead, these were rigid rulebooks that dictated the next move. One such algorithm was created by Alan Turing jointly with his friend David Champernowne and another by two Bletchley Park alumni, Donald Michie and Shaun Wylie. It is said that the Michie-Wylie 'virtual machine', named Machiavelli,

challenged the Turing-Champernowne effort, named TuroChamp, to a match. Each move involved hours of slogging over the algorithm with pencil and paper, the outcome of which was sent to the opponents in the post. It is not recorded who won.

When Alan Turing reached Manchester, the idea of the thinking machine became well and truly sensationalized, with a newspaper article claiming that the computer was a 'brain' with astonishing powers.

Let's put this in perspective. While Alan Turing was asserting that the electronic brain at Manchester was going to compete with humans on equal terms, the reality was that he was talking about the machine in the 'Magnetism Room' whose memory size was 1,024 binary digits. Nevertheless, the achievement that *The Times* described was a genuine world first: on 21 June 1948, the Manchester computer had run the world's first program on a stored-program electronic computing machine. And it caught the public imagination – or, at least, the idea of a thinking

THE TIMES, SATURDAY JUNE 11 1949
THE MECHANICAL BRAIN
ANSWER FOUND TO 300 YEAR-OLD SUM
FROM OUR SPECIAL CORRESPONDENT

Experiments which have seen progress in this country and the United States since the end of the war to produce an efficient mechanical 'brain' have been successfully completed at Manchester University, where a workable 'brain' has been evolved ... It has just completed, in a matter of weeks, a problem, the nature of which is not disclosed, which was started in the 17th century and is only just being completed by human calculation...

Mr. Turing said yesterday: *'This is only a foretaste of what is to come, and only the shadow of what is going to be. We have to have some experience with the machine before we really know its capabilities. It may take years before we settle down to the new possibilities, but I do not see why it should not enter any one of the fields normally covered by the human intellect, and eventually compete on equal terms.'*

machine did. Despite the very mathematical nature of the undisclosed 17th-century problem, computing had escaped from the grasp of the numerical analysts and

The Manchester Small-Scale Experimental Machine, also known as the Manchester Baby, was the world's first stored-program computer.

become a question of the capabilities of an artificial brain.

Despairing of language

The immediate consequences were that Alan Turing, his boss Max Newman and various others were exposed to the media spotlight; when the fuss had died down, the enduring question remained: could a machine actually be said to think? While for Alan Turing the answer was obvious, on the opposing side, also from Manchester, was Sir Geoffrey Jefferson, the country's leading expert on surgery of the brain, who argued that:

No mechanism could feel (and not merely artificially signal, an easy contrivance) pleasure at its successes, grief when its valves fuse, be warmed by flattery, be made miserable by its mistakes, be charmed by sex, be angry or depressed when it cannot get what it wants ... I see a new and greater danger threatening – that of anthropomorphizing the machine. When we hear it said that wireless valves think, we may despair of language.

300-YEAR-OLD SUM

The program that made the headline in *The Times* in June 1949 was not the first one to run on the Manchester Baby computer. That honour belonged to a factorization routine that, on 21 June 1948, successfully found that the highest factor of 262,144 is 131,072 (that is 131,072 ÷ 2 = 262,144; therefore showing that 2 and 131,072 are factors of 262,144). It took 52 minutes and did not bring earth-shattering mathematical news to a waiting population. A simple enough maths question, but it was a historical moment: the first program run on an electronic stored-program computer anywhere in the world and because the human operators knew the answer already, they knew the program had worked.

The 21 June program proved nothing except that the machine worked. However, even the Baby – a huge roomful of equipment despite its nickname – could work on a problem where the answer was not yet known. This was the '300-year-old sum'. The French mathematician Marin Mersenne (1588–1648) posed various questions about numbers taking the form $2^n - 1$, many of which are *prime* (a prime number is divisible by one and itself but no other whole number). One of those questions is: for which values of n are the numbers prime numbers? Working this out with pencil and paper for large values of n is, shall we say, tedious. Since the year 1876 ($n = 127$) no higher numbers had been cracked, although Mersenne had $n = 67$ (not correct) and $n = 257$ (not known) on his list of primes.

Testing Mersenne primes up to $n = 257$ had been carefully selected by Max Newman to run on his limited-memory machine because the Mersenne primes take the form 111111111... in binary, which was (in Newman's words) 'a very nice thing for the computer'. It took 300 years and 1024 bits to show that Mersenne was wrong: $2^{257} - 1$ is not prime. Sorry.

Marin Mersenne was a French mathematician who developed the Mersenne prime numbers, which can be calculated by the formula $2^n - 1$.

MARIN MERSENNE

There was plenty of debate to be had, some of it between Jefferson and Turing on the wireless.

Turing had a further opportunity to tease out the question in a paper he wrote for the journal *Mind* in 1950. In this, he disposes of various arguments put (by Jefferson among others and even referring to Ada, the Countess of Lovelace) against the idea of thinking machines. And, famously, he sets out an imitation test that you can apply to see if a machine is really thinking. This – the 'Turing Test' – envisages two contestants, one human and one machine, and a human judge, who is out of sight and hearing; and by a simple process of question and answer the judge has to ascertain which of the contestants is which. If the judge can't tell,

---

THE LOVE LETTERS WERE FAKES

When the Manchester Baby computer was replaced by a full-size machine, it included a random number generator. This feature had an unexpected result. Visitors to the computer lab at Manchester found love letters pinned to the noticeboard; surely inappropriate for such intimate material.

Darling Moppet,

My devotion holds dear your infatuation. My fervour treasures your affection. You are my beautiful wish. My amorous wish covetously hopes for your tender eagerness. You are my avid fellow feeling.

Yours tenderly,

M.U.C.

Darling Love,

You are my sweet ardour. My loving fondness covetously pants for your precious being. My yearning fondly pants for your tender little liking. You are my burning heart, my burning ardour.

Yours fondly,

M.U.C.

Could computers love? Love letters were found pinned to the Manchester University Computer Laboratory's noticeboard, supposedly written by the computer itself.

It was down to Christopher Strachey, who had put the random-number generator to a novel use. After you've read two or three you get the idea and their charm begins to wear thin; and the insiders will have guessed quickly that M.U.C. stands for Manchester University Computer. But, for all their frivolity, they showed something important: with only a limited degree of sophistication, for just a short while they might take you in; they might look like real letters. It's not surprising that Sir Geoffrey Jefferson was arguing that computing and feelings should have nothing to do with each other.

then the machine is thinking. Below is an example of the kind of convincing dialogue that Alan Turing thought might take place.

The Turing Test can be criticized on a number of grounds, though it still generates a good deal of interest with prizes on offer.

Interrogator: In the first line of your sonnet which reads 'Shall I compare thee to a summer's day', would not 'a spring day' do as well or better?

Witness: It wouldn't scan.

Interrogator: How about a 'winter's day'. That would scan all right.

Witness: Yes, but nobody wants to be compared to a winter's day.

Interrogator: Would you say Mr. Pickwick reminded you of Christmas?

Witness: In a way.

Interrogator: Yet Christmas is a winter's day, and I do not think Mr. Pickwick would mind the comparison.

Witness: I don't think you're serious. By a winter's day one means a typical winter's day, rather than a special one like Christmas.

TURING TEST TODAY

The Loebner prize was instituted in 1990. It offered $100,000 and a gold medal for the first computer whose responses were indistinguishable from a human's. The gold medal has never been awarded. Instead, each year a smaller cash prize and a bronze medal is awarded to the computer most closely approximating a human. In addition to the Loebner contest, other competitions and events are run periodically in which software is pitted against humans in some version of the imitation game.

Academics dismiss the Loebner prize as irrelevant and a distraction from serious work on artificial intelligence. The academics may be right to argue that the Turing Test is archaic and asking the wrong question in a modern context. Whether something or someone 'thinks' is – as Sir Geoffrey Jefferson was saying back in 1949 – to ask whether someone is human, since we cannot strip off from the word the layers of clothing and connotations that result from millennia of applying the concept to people.

Hugh Loebner, an American inventor and entrepreneur, set up the Loebner prize for programmers who could create an AI that could pass the Turing Test.

Despite the criticism, the easy to understand nature of the Turing Test means that it continues to appeal to a wide public. Every so often a chatbot or other program gets some media attention (including predictable 'it's all nonsense' reactions from academics) by fooling judges in one of the world's regular Turing Test competitions. Artificial intelligence researchers don't tend to assess the effectiveness of their discoveries by reference to the Turing Test. As Edsger Dijkstra said in 1984, 'The question of whether machines can think is about as relevant as the question of whether submarines can swim.' It's just too artificial.

For true artificial existence to exist, machines would have to learn themselves, rather than rely on the direct inputs of their programmers.

We are then faced with the problem of finding suitable branches of thought for the machine to exercise its powers in. The following fields appear to me to have advantages:
(i) Various games, e.g., chess, noughts and crosses, bridge, poker
(ii) The learning of languages
(iii) Translation of languages
(iv) Cryptography
(v) Mathematics.

Alan Turing, 'Intelligent Machinery' (1948).

A more analytical approach to what constitutes 'intelligent' machinery can be found in another paper of Turing's, written when he took a year's sabbatical leave in 1947 to give freer rein to his absurd ideas about 'intelligent' machinery than was possible in the staid Mathematics Division of the NPL. During his year away, Turing's vision of computing machinery's capabilities was put on to paper. 'Intelligent' machines should be capable of learning from their mistakes and displaying creativity. To develop these traits a machine would have to be 'un-organized', in the sense of contrasting its behaviour with that of 'organized' machines that run, tram-like, according to pre-ordained grooves set by their programmer. If machines are to be intelligent, rather than automata, they must be allowed to make mistakes: 'if a machine is expected to be infallible, it cannot also be intelligent'.

When Turing first proposed his paper, the idea of machines translating a language seemed preposterous. Today, it is an everyday occurrence.

Bearing in mind that, when this was written in 1947, the first program had not been run on any computer anywhere, it must have seemed delirious. The very idea of a machine that could learn or translate a language! Everybody knew that it was the limit of a machine's capability to process arithmetical operations. Alan Turing's paper on intelligent machinery was buried by the NPL and did not get published until after his death, by which time artificial intelligence had become established as a legitimate field of study.

In the meantime, research into machine learning and other ways in which machines might demonstrate intelligence needed to await the development of computers with, well, sufficient computing power.

Brain training

Computing is supposed to comprise operations that happen in sequence, whereas cognitive processes don't happen like that: except that Alan Turing had ideas for circuitry

---

TURING'S NEURONS

Central to the concept of a 'teachable' machine is to convert its 'un-organized' state to an organized one 'by suitable interfering training'. You can get this result using the Boolean operator NAND, which is the mirror-image of AND:

a	b	a AND b	a NAND b
1	1	1	0
1	0	0	1
0	1	0	1
0	0	0	1

If you regard input 'a' as being the teacher and input 'b' as the pupil, a '0' input from the teacher will cancel the input of the pupil altogether; a '1' input from the teacher allows the pupil's input to go through. (Using the notation of Claude Shannon for circuitry, a '0' represents a closed switch, where electricity flows, and a '1' an open switch.)

The McCulloch-Pitts idea is that a nerve cell has a single output, as many excitatory and inhibitory inputs as you like and an activation threshold. An inhibitory input prevents any output. If there is no inhibition and the excitatory inputs (which could build up over time) exceed the threshold the output fires. You can now start connecting these synthetic nerve cells to perform Boolean logical functions: AND, OR and NOT can be done with a single 'neuron'; XOR requires several.

Learning can also happen. For this to work you need to be able to change the strength of the input signal through feedback. If you know what you're aiming for, you can alter the strength by measuring how far off target the output was. With repeated iterations, the neural model gets closer to the desired output.

The work of Warren McCulloch and Walter Pitts noticed the parallels between the neurons of the human brain and the way in which circuits could be used for logical operations.

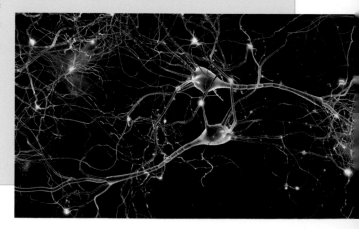

Dartmouth College held a conference on artificial intelligence in 1956. It established AI as a major field of study and set the course for the development of 'thinking machines'.

that could actually allow an 'un-organized machine' to modify its behaviour based on experience; or, in more homely terms, to be 'rewarded' or 'punished' for good or bad outcomes. Circuits linked together into an artificial 'neural network' – modelled, more or less, on the complex synapse structure of human brains – are the structural device through which machines are trained. The more layers there are in the network the deeper the learning that is possible.

It might seem a thoroughly daunting idea to try to dissect the brain with its billions of neural connections, but in 1943 Warren McCulloch and Walter Pitts had explained in a paper that neurophysiology could be equated to circuitry and logic gates. Brain cells accept inputs that may be excitatory or inhibitory and fire an impulse to their output synapses when the excitements reach a given threshold; by connecting the cells into nets one finds that the nets are capable of carrying out computable functions, in the manner of a Turing machine. Logical operations can

be done by networks of neurons. Logic operations in the brain could be like logic operations in a computer; computers could learn.

In the mid-1950s enough thinking had been done (by humans) for a technical conference on artificial intelligence, which took place in Dartmouth, New Hampshire, in 1956. The show was stolen by a program that could prove theorems described in the definitive work on fundamental mathematical principles by Alfred North Whitehead and Bertrand Russell, published in three volumes in 1910, 1912 and 1913 and titled *Principia Mathematica*, in an allusion to another work of the same name by none other than Sir Isaac Newton. The program showed that it was feasible to get a machine to reason deductively: that is, from axioms to a conclusion. But what about inductive reasoning, the more creative aspects of intelligence? Much of the research on artificial intelligence since then has been channelled into this, the other side of thinking.

Inductive reasoning is naturally fuzzy and that's part of the reason why it did not immediately fit with the tram-track programming of computers designed for mathematical computation. To imagine, or create, or recognize, you need to make do with mathematically incomplete generalizations, extrapolations and guesswork. It's easier to learn if you do not apply excessive zeal to categorizing things (not all cats are black, not all houses have pointy roofs, and so on). All of this sounds wholly incompatible with the processes of an electronic computer – until you recall that the Bombe, the machine built to find Enigma settings in World War II, was a fuzzy-logic machine, finding a selection of possible answers rather than a mathematically precise proof of a theorem. To put it another way, searching is non-deterministic.

'Programs with common sense', to adopt the words of the computer scientist John McCarthy in 1958, would use knowledge to search for solutions and could accept new ideas without being reprogrammed. Intelligence and reaction to the environment are interwoven, so intelligent machinery needs to learn, make observations, classify, react to unexperienced elements of its environment and adapt to changed circumstances.

In 1997, the World Chess Champion took on the IBM computer Deep Blue and lost. Since then, machines have overtaken humans in the field of chess.

GO FOR IT

In March 2016, an artificial intelligence system called AlphaGo developed by Google beat its human opponent, the world champion of the Japanese board game Go. Go is regarded as being one of the most challenging games for a machine to succeed at – a lot tougher than chess. The system's success in March 2016 was because of a very unusual move – a highly creative one – which initially caused concern that the algorithm had malfunctioned. Not so. But while the world champion can explain how his own playing style has been influenced by the machine's clever move, the machine cannot explain to us how it came upon the idea.

Go is a far more challenging game than chess, relying much more on intuition than logic. In March 2016 the computer system AlphaGo beat the world champion by using a move that humans had not foreseen.

Artificial ideas

Several things have happened since the first tentative steps to create artificial intelligence. Chess-playing algorithms are now regarded as somewhat passé, ever since the program Deep Blue beat the grandmaster Garry Kasparov by 3½–2½ in 1997. Deep Blue was hardly an intelligent device. The way it worked was to look as far ahead as possible (typically six to eight moves ahead) and choose the optimal move. It did this using parallel processors to work through the permutations, drawing on a library of expert knowledge gleaned from experienced grandmasters to evaluate the options. More modern algorithms do not depend solely on brute force; humans engaged in problem-solving try out wacky and unorthodox possibilities and learn by experience and this machine-learning model has been incorporated into a range of intelligent systems with success.

'Expert systems' (such as the library of grandmasters' expertise) were, for a while, regarded as manifestations of intelligence in machines. Complex programs were developed to follow the logical paths taken by expert humans in complex decision-making processes, such as design, diagnosis and problem-solving. But expert systems are not intelligent unless they can adapt to unforeseen situations: to show intelligence something more than 'mechanical' behaviour

René Descartes posed his own test for machine intelligence 300 years before Turing.

disciplines, stand-offs between advocates of different theories. Machine learning is currently where it's at. Big data, search engines, natural language processing, interactive maps – anything you can think of that is 'smart technology' is likely to have a machine learning algorithm at its centre. What makes human brains better at learning than machines is based around recognition and selection: sifting out peripheral and irrelevant clutter. Merely knowing lots of facts does not make it easier to know which ones are relevant. Machine learning is constrained, because computers sample only a limited range of world experiences.

Some research is directed at designing AI systems that attempt to mimic the brain in a physical as well as a functional sense. The first step in this is to deconstruct the brain. With 100 billion neurons, each of which makes 7,000 synaptic connections with other neurons, this might be described as a challenge. So the scientists started with a nematode worm, *Caenorhabditis elegans*, whose brain has 302 neurons, and it was completely mapped in 1986. Superb, but it is rather less informative than the complete sequencing of the human genome: deconstructing the wiring tells us very little about the software it is running.

Much research into artificial intelligence is aimed at specific functions. For example, in the United States, research funding has been made available in recent years for application of algorithms to healthcare,

is needed. If we are to avoid contradicting ourselves, this raises a question about what we mean by 'mechanical'. René Descartes wrote about this as long ago as 1637 in his *Discours de la Méthode*. He even posed the Turing Test:

> 'We may easily conceive a machine constructed so that it utters words, and even that it utters some which correspond to the action upon it ... although such machines might execute many things with equal or perhaps greater perfection than any of us, they would, without doubt, fail in others from which it could be discovered that they did not act from knowledge.'

There have been 'AI winters' – periods when researchers thought they were getting nowhere – and, as with many academic

The IBM computer Watson even participated on the gameshow Jeopardy *in 2011 and won comfortably. Since then it has been engaged in more valuable pursuits, including cancer diagnosis, tutoring and forecasting the weather.*

security, advertising and finance as well as the development of general-purpose artificial intelligence technology.

Specific research projects also focus on computer vision, natural language processing, robotics, machine learning, computation and 'modelling of intelligence in complex, realistic contexts'. Or, to put it more concisely, a lot of research money was, in 2016, being spent on self-driving cars.

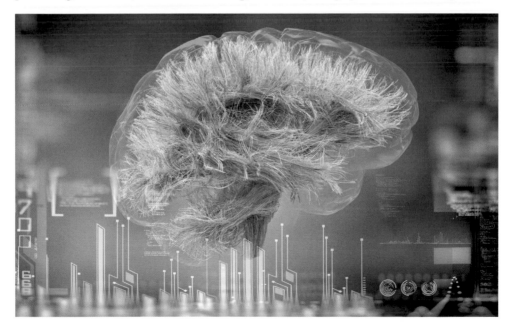

To achieve artificial intelligence, we must first understand the human brain. Consisting of 100 billion neurons, and even more synaptic connections, it is a daunting challenge.

BEEN THERE, DONE THAT

Pittsburgh, Pennsylvania, 1994. 'Research scientist Dean Pomerleau and robotics doctoral student Todd Jochem won't touch the steering wheel but they will operate the throttle and brakes of a 1990 Pontiac,' proclaimed the Carnegie Mellon hype. The car did its own steering, based on a 30×32 pixel 'vision' of the road ahead, and a neural network program run on a processor that was the size of an Intel 486DX2. Some 2,797 miles later the Pontiac rolled into San Diego, California. Nowadays, people driving across America use cruise control and GPS – so they do the steering but don't use the throttle or their own direction-finding. You can debate the merits of each approach, but the 1994 version had one edge over a modern rented motor-home: 'We have a really cool T-shirt to commemorate the trip.'

The first self-driving car hit the road in 1994. Dean Pomerleau and Todd Jochem made the nerve-wracking 2,797-mile journey across America without touching the steering wheel.

Artificial intelligence can be regarded as a moving target – in other words, what we are accustomed to having machines do ceases to be regarded as 'intelligent' behaviour and is swept aside as purely 'mechanical' as soon as we get used to it. Optical recognition and language translation programs are an example of this.

Running alongside research into artificial intelligence has been the development of robotics. Robotics is primarily concerned with combining sensory systems with feedback mechanisms so that machines can sense their environment and their place within it and adjust their actions accordingly. For example, much research has been done in industrial robotics to build machines that can be harnessed to a conveyor belt and – just as humans do now – recognise and assemble components as they come by. Cars are now produced that can parallel park without human intervention and may soon be able to drive around town and in traffic while their human passengers sit back and enjoy the ride.

The bar for artificial intelligence keeps being raised. Behaviour such as facial recognition was once considered intelligent. Now that machines can do it too, it is seen as purely mechanical.

The real step change in robotics will come, however, when these automatic systems can be linked to AI to produce humanoid robots – machines able to learn, make mistakes and learn from them, adapt to changing situations, and so act independently to carry out jobs that previously only a human could do.

The rise of the robot

It is a curious thing that, for many centuries, humans have been fascinated by artificial people: automata androids and the like. The fascination is explained partly by curiosity, as they engender both humour and alarm in equal measure. Early automata were symbols of prestige, since only the mighty could afford the precision-engineering and years of design work needed to create an automaton. The automata of the 18th and 19th centuries had marvellous, almost magical, abilities. French inventors in particular excelled at these intricate constructions, such as Jacques de Vaucanson's flute-playing statue, or the letter-writing doll of Pierre Jaquet-Droz.

Automata like Pierre Jaquet-Droz's letter-writing doll were engineering marvels, but they did not reflect true intelligence.

But it is hard to escape the idea that these automata had ever been much more than expensive, amusing, cutesy toys. They do not serve any higher purpose. What they lacked, moreover, was flexibility. They were hard-wired into patterns of behaviour that seem natural at first, but which tarnish after several viewings. And they were fixed, until the self-propelled automaton became engineering reality in the first half of the 20th century.

Rossum

There's an enduring myth about the origin of the term 'robot': it is attributed to the Czech writer Karel Čapek, whose 1920 play *R.U.R.* (or *Rossumovi univerzálni roboti*) was a sensation. In *R.U.R.*, an inventor called

TIPU'S TIGER

As the war between Britain and France rolled on across Europe and at sea following the French Revolution, the two countries began scrapping for control in India. One local potentate, Sultan Fateh Ali Sahab Tipu, known as 'the tiger of Mysore', sided with the French. He commissioned from his French allies a masterpiece of automaton

engineering, a mechanical tiger that when set in motion would maul a British serviceman (also, thankfully, part of the automaton).

Tipu's Tiger is a mechanical tiger mauling a British serviceman, a gift from his French allies.

The tiger would growl while it mangled its prey.

Regrettably for Tipu Sultan, one of his military opponents was a young officer called Arthur Wellesley. Tipu was beaten decisively by Wellesley at the Battle of Seringatapam in 1799 and his tiger is now in the Victoria and Albert Museum in London.

Sultan Fateh Ali Sahab Tipu was known as 'the tiger of Mysore' and sided with the French against the British in the late 18th century.

A toy robot stands on the grave of Karel Čapek, the man responsible for the modern usage of the word 'robot'.

Britain and America and the term 'robot' became associated with human-like machines.

The Cybermen

A new field of scientific study has grown out of the robot idea. This is the study of 'control and communication in the animal and the machine', or to use the word invented for this field, cybernetics. Cybernetics was the brain-child of the American mathematician Norbert Wiener, and cybernetics is all about computing.

Norbert Wiener's choice of name for the discipline he founded was not random. 'The name *Cybernetics* we form from the Greek χυβερνήτης or *steersman*.' It was all about

Rossum (which means 'reason' in Czech) creates a sort of half-machine, half-person that can carry out tasks ordinarily given to low-paid workers. The machines are churned out by the thousand in a huge factory, fulfilling orders from all around the world. Things begin to go wrong when the design of the machines is modified to give them personality.

In Slavic languages, 'robot' and its cognates are from an old root word from which worker, slave, serf, factory and so forth derive. When Čapek's play was translated into English it became a roaring success in

The Cybermen of Doctor Who *reflected the new fascination with robots.*

governors: not bosses, but the feedback mechanisms found on steam engines in 1948, when Wiener was writing.

Cybernetics begins with the question of how a creature – let's say a dog – senses its environment and issues to its motor organs appropriate signals – let's say, to avoid running into a wall. In the late 1940s, when Wiener issued his seminal book on cybernetics, analogous problems were being addressed by computer scientists – how a computing machine adapts its behaviour in response to different inputs. Formally, these seemed to be similar questions. In 1950 in Britain, a group comprising biologists, mathematicians and computer scientists and calling themselves the Ratio Club began to meet to debate these ideas.

As to command and control, Wiener explained that it's all about feedback: continuously modifying a movement in progress so as to improve the result; so, if (to use his example) he wants to pick up a pencil, he does not 'perform the act by a conscious willing in succession of the contraction of each muscle concerned' but by a feedback process to do with keeping an eye on the pencil. Moreover, the whole process is outside the doer's consciousness.

Wiener saw a machine that McCulloch had built to scan printed words and read

Norbert Wiener was the father of cybernetics and formalized the idea of feedback.

them out – a machine built in 1947 – and remarked that another academic had asked if a diagram of the apparatus was 'a diagram of the fourth layer of the visual cortex of the brain.' So the control of robotic behaviour is, in fact, a form of computing; robots can learn; and the tendency of people to mix up the disciplines of cybernetics and artificial intelligence can be excused.

What emerges from the early forays into robotics is that programmable, mobile automata can have apparently complex behaviours driven from very simple algorithms. One member of the Ratio Club, Grey Walter, had a pair of tortoises, called Elsie and Elmer. They would run

BIG BROTHER

Britain was worried. The House of Commons Science and Technology Committee decided to examine robotics and artificial intelligence 'after the Government was unable to produce a short statement outlining the evidence underpinning its policy on artificial intelligence'. In 2016 the Committee's report was published, covering social, ethical and legal questions as well as criticism of government policy. The Committee noted that one witness had said 'there is no AI without robotics'. Understandable, but wrong. Only if the machine roaming around is endowed with intelligence have the two concepts merged. There is plenty of AI and there are plenty of robots; though to watch you, Big Brother (in the Orwellian sense) needed only one of those capabilities.

around and apparently explore, negotiate obstacles, head towards the light and return to the hutch for an energy boost. As with all small creatures on public display, the people adored them. What gave it away was the sign above the hutch: 'Please do not feed these machines.' For Elsie and Elmer were little robots.

Received wisdom in 1950 held that artificial brains would require huge numbers of valves and immense amounts of electricity. However, the tortoises' motors were controlled using only two 'nerve cell units' comprising one electronic

valve each and two sensors (a photoelectric cell and a touch-sensor); Walter reckoned they were demonstrating seven types of behaviour.

The two tortoise-like robots designed by William Grey Walter, Elsie and Elmer, could explore their environments and avoid obstacles. They needed only two 'nerve cell units' to do this.

INKHA

If you went into the reception area of King's College, London, before 2015, you might have been greeted by Inkha. She had a camera in her eye and watched the visitors. If there wasn't anything to look at she dozed off. If you flapped at her suddenly she would look alarmed. She would also give directions, dispense fashion tips and flutter her eyelashes. Alas, for those thinking of asking the receptionist for a date, she was little more than a talking head.

When Inkha retired, she was replaced by Kinba, who can hear as well as see and is said to tell jokes. Kinba has learning ability too and is probably a better receptionist. But she's green and globular and that doesn't put her very high up in the robotic glamour chart.

Inkha the Robot worked as a receptionist at King's College, London, before 2015 and was able to express emotions, give advice and provide information.

Although more modern robots are designed to have human-like characteristics, to learn from their experiences, even to be human emulators, they still might seem to offer little more than the automata of previous centuries.

Day of the drones

Human lookalikes and emulators may be a distraction from the serious business of computing. Other types of robot may not capture the attention of movie-goers but may have more influence on our lives.

Drones now do many of the jobs deemed too dangerous for humans. Disarming unexploded bombs is much safer for a human operator many miles away.

These are the '4D' robots – the ones that do tasks that are Dull, Dumb, Dirty and Dangerous. They do routine, precision jobs in factories. They check out suspect premises and disarm unexploded bombs. And they include unmanned weapons.

Unless you are the target of a camera-carrying or bomb-dropping drone, the industrial robot may not pose a great threat. It is perhaps remarkable, though maybe a consequence of the apparent innocuousness of industrial and human-like robots, that it

THREE LAWS

I, Robot (2004) is the film re-creation of ideas in a story collection by the science fiction writer Isaac Asimov in 1942. Robots in the film are supposed to obey the Three Laws:

- A robot may not injure a human being or, through inaction, allow a human being to come to harm.
- A robot must obey orders given to it by human beings, except where such orders would conflict with the First Law.
- A robot must protect its own existence as long as such protection does not conflict with the First or Second Law.

In 1985, Asimov broadened the concept to look at the way robots might influence society as a whole and proposed a fourth law to run before the other three – called the Zeroth Law:

- A robot may not harm humanity, or by inaction, allow humanity to come to harm.

Isaac Asimov proposed three laws of robotics in a story, later filmed as 'I, Robot' to protect humans from the dangers of AI.

has been left to a science fiction writer – admittedly one of the all-time greats – to specify the ethical rules that ought to apply to cybernetics. Even a leading university-level textbook on artificial intelligence cites Isaac Asimov's 'Three Rules', without suggesting any alternative. (Another academic writer believes that Asimov's rules were deliberately formulated with rough edges in order to provide scope for great storylines and dramatic tension – in other words, that they are not at all the code of laws that they might at first seem.)

In 1959, the British inventor Gordon

UNFINISHED SYMPHONY

Among the parallels between the lives of two of the founding fathers of computer science – Alan Turing and John von Neumann – is that they both died young, with unfinished work on their desks. In both cases, the origins of their unfinished work related to cybernetics. In the case of von Neumann, it was the theory of self-replicating automata: what was mathematically necessary for robots to inherit the earth. In the case of Alan Turing, the stimulus given by talking in the Ratio Club about control in living things had set him in a new direction – morphogenesis, or the development of growth and form in animals and plants, and the search for a mathematical or chemical explanation for the patterns seen in nature. Both these mathematicians had been computing for life.

Alan Turing used the computer at Manchester University to model the concentration of chemicals during the process of morphogenesis. He translated the numerical read-out into a kind of map to show how spots might form on an animal skin.

The 'M-blocks' are modular robotic cubes that can move, climb and group together.

Pask assembled an electrochemical system that developed metallic threads in a bath of electrolyte. The threads could learn a successful pattern and rapidly re-establish it if their environment was disrupted, could be trained to discriminate between different sounds and exhibit other lifelike behaviours. Things have not stood still since then.

M-block

Today, robots come in all shapes and sizes. M-blocks are 'modular robots'. They don't look like proper humanoid robots from science fiction. In fact, according to MIT, 'the robots are cubes with no external moving parts. Nonetheless, they're able to climb over and around one another, leap through the air, roll across the ground and even move while suspended upside down from metallic surfaces.' They appear to play around together and to be able to assemble into groupings, aligning neatly one against another. The mechanism that achieves this is 'surprisingly simple': a flywheel inside each cube, which imparts its angular momentum to the cube when the brake is applied. There are also magnets on the cubes that allow them to attach to each other. MIT's information about M-blocks goes on to say 'the hope is that the modules can be miniaturized: the ultimate aim of most such research is hordes of swarming microbots that can self-assemble, like the "liquid steel" androids in the movie "Terminator II."'

Chapter 10

COMPUTING THE FUTURE

The transformations of society wrought by technological developments have been debated for half a century. Threats are seen in that traditional jobs are assumed by intelligent machines. Quantum computers might become a reality, endangering privacy protection, or possibly making it more secure.

Computing will shape our future as much as it has our past. Whether on expeditions to Mars or in our own homes, computing presents both immense opportunities and new dangers.

Artificial intelligence, cybernetics, cryptography, big data: the 21st century has computing concepts that were barely imagined a hundred years ago and which many now believe may govern our lives.

The issue today is not so much that the robot (or the artificial intelligence or whatever other computing development happens to be in the news) ate your job – that is unavoidable – but what jobs will replace the one that has been eaten. The lament in official circles is that we lack 'digital skills' among our workforce. (Maybe this is because we were complacent immediately after the computing revolution: teaching of computing in schools became teaching of 'ICT', which cynics would say was nothing more complicated than helping the teacher understand how to access his email. Now we have begun to do it properly again.)

The transformation of the economy

Klaus Schwab is the founder of the World Economic Forum and has claimed that we are now in the throes of a fourth industrial revolution.

is being described as the fourth industrial revolution. According to Klaus Schwab, founder and chairman of the World Economic Forum, we are now experiencing a fourth industrial revolution, characterized by 'a fusion of technologies that is blurring the lines between the physical, digital and biological spheres'.

Another, more subtle, variant of the 'robot ate my job' concern is that artificial intelligence is destroying lower-skilled jobs, leaving an important demographic with little future. A world where social care and logistics roles are taken over by intelligent socially aware robots and self-driving cars may seem dystopian, but can we replace those jobs with other, more fulfilling ones?

There is a real fear that robots and artificial intelligences will take our jobs. But the important question is what are the jobs that will replace those taken over by machines.

- The mathematician G.H. Hardy said, in the dark days of a world war, 'A science is said to be useful if its development tends to accentuate the existing inequalities in the distribution of wealth, or more directly promotes the destruction of human life.' Most people would protest that, but a more serious underlying message is how scientific research is funded and towards what end. Commercial and military exploitation have not gone away. Artificial intelligences will absorb these objectives, whether overtly or covertly stated.

Ray Kurzweil, a leading American futurist and proponent of the idea of the 'Singularity', has an optimistic view of the role AI can play in the future.

- 'The idea of non-human devices of great power and great ability to carry through a policy, and of their dangers, is nothing new,' wrote Norbert Wiener in 1948. His book, *Cybernetics: Or Control and Communication in the Animal and the Human Machine*, reminded readers in a cautionary way about the Sorcerer's Apprentice and the Monkey's Paw; 'In all these stories the point is that the agencies of magic are literal-minded; and that if we ask a boon from them, we must ask for what we really want and not for what we think we want.' Wiener also said, 'It may very well be a good thing for humanity to have the machine remove from it the need of menial and disagreeable tasks, or it may not. I do not know.'

- In 1976, Alvin Toffler wrote a book called *Future Shock* that warned of the culture shock that people would suffer in a world whose technological change happened faster than their ability to adapt. He also predicted, 'The work week has been cut by 50 per cent since the turn of the century. It is not out of the way to predict that it will be slashed in half again by 2000.' The idea that technology is going to make couch-potatoes of us all may be overblown.

Some don't see any of this as a threat, but an opportunity to be seized. The American writer, thinker and inventor Ray Kurzweil, in particular, thinks that the combination of 'GNR' (genetics, nanotechnology, robotics) technologies will enable people to live forever and enjoy life in unimagined (to us) but different ways. What's going to happen, according to Kurzweil, is a simultaneous spike – growth so fast we cannot see it happen – in development in these areas. This could be all for the good, if we wake up and ride the wave, or it could be doom and disaster. Where exponential change is happening so fast it becomes a spike, we lose control; Kurzweil calls this point the 'singularity'.

S IS FOR SPIKE

The same data presented three ways.

As the series begins, growth appears to be linear.

But as time goes by, a different pattern appears: growth is actually exponential, or so it seems. There looks to be a spike developing.

Except that exponential growth can tail off, as limiting factors come into play, turning the spike into an S-curve.

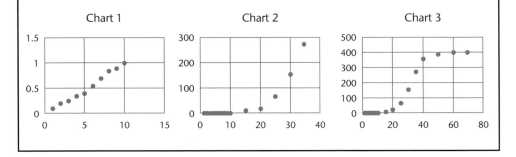

Chart 1   Chart 2   Chart 3

Superbrain

Particularly as regards artificial intelligence, it seems readily imaginable that an intelligent machine – or rather, a combination of intelligent algorithms – will acquire 'super-intelligence' and that that might happen in a manner that behaves like a singularity. Super-intelligence is not just being better than us at something (like pattern-spotting or searching a database, which existing algorithms already do far better than humans) but at everything and without the burdens of our animal existence to hold them back in a cage of 'irrationality' (or, if you prefer, humanity).

Some wonder what will happen when we get to that stage, fearing an environment in which super-intelligent non-biological entities take over.

The development of super-intelligence is probably inevitable. Debate rages about when machines will develop intelligence that is both superior to human intelligence and general. (We already have artificial

---

The statistician I.J. Good – a friend and colleague of Alan Turing and an alumnus of Bletchley Park – wrote in 1965:

Let an ultraintelligent machine be defined as a machine that can far surpass all the intellectual activities of any man however clever. Since the design of machines is one of these intellectual activities, an ultraintelligent machine could design even better machines; there would then unquestionably be an 'intelligence explosion', and the intelligence of man would be left far behind.

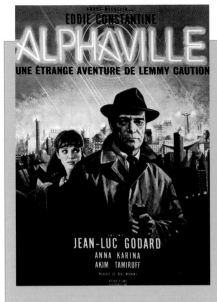

The 1965 movie Alphaville *featured an all-powerful computer and a brainwashed population. It reflects many of our fears of super-intelligent machines.*

ALPHAVILLE

Jean-Luc Godard's movies tend to be strange, but none is stranger than *Alphaville* (1965). As well as being a satire on contemporary authoritarian cultures, with brainwashed people who behave like automata and a central, powerful computer that controls everything, *Alphaville* has curious allusions to all sorts of things covered in this book. There is an Institute of Semantics, symbolic logic, the number 60, secret messages and even a reference to insect society. The ideas of *Alphaville* have spawned a column in the *Financial Times*, German and Swedish pop groups, a designer fashion label, computer-geek websites and more. The film also features robotic girls whose occupation is said to be 'Level Three Seductress', but there are some aspects of Godard filmology that cannot be fitted politely into a book about computing.

intelligences that are superior in specific, narrow, fields, but a cash liquidity management system in a bank is not going to have the capability to take over the planet, despite conspiracy theories about international banking.)

More soberly, some observations about super-human artificial intelligence can be made:

- The House of Commons Science and Technology Committee issued a report in October 2016 that pinpointed some of the fears and concerns around artificial intelligence. Some fear that automation will cause the loss of jobs and what will remain for humans to do if machines become more creative. Others fear the speed of change and a moment at which a cross-over point

– where machine intelligence becomes so superior to human intelligence that it can improve and self-modify so fast that there is then nothing humans could do to stop what they have unleashed. Other concerns included loss of privacy, bias, inadequately controlled automated weapons and legal liability. On the other side of the debate is an expectation that automation increases productivity and provides opportunities for new and higher-quality jobs.

- Regulation of developing artificial intelligence is thus important. The House of Commons report emphasized the need for verification and validation of new artificial systems before deployment, development of kill-switches to zap a new system before it could learn how to avoid or manipulate the switch, as well as governance and decision-making structures.

- A cross-over to 'super-intelligence' may be inevitable, but the debate is confused. You might pooh-pooh the idea that this would threaten humans, because to carry out a take-over, in some neo-Marxist way, of the means of production, distribution and exchange, something more than a piece of software is needed. Movement, replication, growth – those aspects of what we call life – appear to be pre-requisites. But there is a danger buried in the debate, which is that a super-intelligence would presumably have different goals from the animal objectives of humans. What those goals might be and how they would develop are matters of speculation. Perhaps, indeed, there may be no algorithm to tell whether another algorithm might go super-intelligent.
- Computers are networked. It is unrealistic to imagine that a super-intelligence could be quelled by pulling out a plug. Furthermore, a super-intelligence would probably be 'distributed' around the network: like a colony of social insects, whose 'person' is not vested in a single individual. 'Superorganisms' are networked, have differentiated roles shared among different agents and have reproductive behaviours which are different from traditional animal patterns. It would be foolhardy to imagine that the solution for controlling a super-intelligent creation is to pull out the plug.

Quantum of solace

If all that is not enough to keep you awake at night, there are other developments being eagerly researched that could increase the power of computing by, literally, a quantum leap. Combining quantum computing with artificial intelligence would undoubtedly transform the power of machines. So what is 'quantum computing'?

The short answer is that it doesn't yet exist, except as a theory. The theory exploits the weird, counter-intuitive behaviour of subatomic particles and light: the ability to be in two places, or two states, at once. Harnessing this enables the parallel-processing ability of computers to be massively increased. It's just a matter of linking up enough quantum-bits (qubits) to handle your problem. In 2001, at MIT, a quantum computer was created with one molecule that

Any super-intelligent machine is likely to be a network of intelligences, like ants, with different roles for different parts of the network.

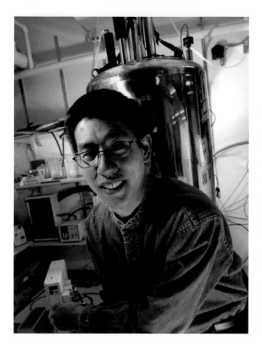

Isaac Chuang stands in front of a quantum computer at MIT. Quantum computers seek to exploit the ability of subatomic particles to be in two places at once.

could be manipulated with nuclear magnetic resonance to factor the number 15. That required 12 qubits. But adding many more atoms, to create assemblies of logic gates to handle more difficult problems, is a nano-engineering problem that has not yet been reliably solved.

When they get there, the number one algorithm on the quantum-computer programmers' list is called Shor's algorithm. The job of this number-cruncher is to reduce to polynomial time our old favourite – the challenge of factorizing a very, very large number into two primes and breaking into the RSA public-key encryption system.

If you can bring on quantum computing, you can also bring on

quantum cryptography, which exploits the same ideas from quantum mechanics. This time the benefits flow from the peculiar behaviour of polarized photons, which (if vertically polarized) can't normally go through a horizontal polaroid filter, but can if allowed to go through one placed at a different angle first. Anyone who tries to parse a message made from a sequence of differently polarized photons will irretrievably ruin the content, so rendering it totally secure to anyone except the intended recipient who can extract a key-string from it.

We have, seemingly, taken a long path away from the Antikythera mechanism and other early devices for measuring the heavens. Except that there is curious parity between the scientific realms of quantum mechanics and the behaviour of celestial things like black holes: the very large and the very small are both very weird. Having come full circle, it is probably time to bring this subject to an end.

A qubit chip like this one can hold up to two states of information (i.e. either 0 or 1) at the same time, unlike traditional processors.

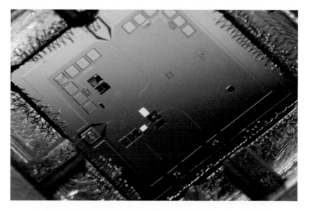

Glossary

Algorithm
steps or rules to be followed in order to make a calculation or solve a problem

Analogue
using continuous measurable quantities to get an answer to a problem – as contrasted with 'digital' methods

ARPANET
the forerunner of the internet, linking institutions funded by the US Department of Defense's Advanced Research Projects Agency (ARPA)

Automaton
a model, often powered by clockwork, which imitates the movement of an animated being

Big Data
all the information which is generated by people using electronic devices – it's not the data that are big, so much as the volume of data that is created

Binary
arithmetic based on only two digits – 1 and 0

Boolean logic
a system, based on the work of George Boole, to determine whether something is a true or false conclusion, which underlies many fundamental computer science ideas – see page 65

Cloud
remote storage of data, accessible via the internet

COBOL
(computer language) COmmon Business-Oriented Language

Compiler
software which interprets a statement in a programming language into instructions which a computer can process

Complement
the number which makes a digit up to 9 for the purpose of subtraction (see page 47)

CRT
cathode ray tube – similar to an old-fashioned television tube, where a beam of electrons is fired at a screen which glows where they hit

Cryptology
discovering the content of secret messages sent in code or cipher

Cybernetics
the study of control of a machine, in particular how it responds to its environment and reacts accordingly

Decidability
the problem of knowing whether a theorem is provable or not

Delay line
technology used as memory in early computing machinery, based on the principle that sound waves travel slowly in a tube of liquid – the delay in the sound wave reaching the end of the tube is what constituted the memory

Digital
using calculated numbers – usually binary numbers – to get an answer to a problem

Electromagnetic relay
when electricity moves in a coil, it generates a magnetic field which can turn an electrical switch on or off.

Encryption
using a code or cipher to conceal the content of a secret message

Exponent
when expressing a long number as a power, the exponent is the piece which is the power (the '5' in 2.993×10^5)

Factorial
multiplication by each smaller whole number : so 6 factorial is $6 \times 5 \times 4 \times 3 \times 2 \times 1 = 720$

FORTRAN
(computer language) FORmula TRANslator

GUI
graphical user interface – showing the output of a computer on its screen as images and icons

LCD
liquid crystal display

Machine learning
where computer programs change their behaviour on the basis of their previous experience – see pages 175–7

Mainframe
large-scale computers typically used in government, academia or business

Malware
'malicious software', received onto a computer with a purpose against the computer user's interest, such as theft, denial of service, coercive purchase etc.

Microprocessor
an entire computer processor embedded in miniature form, typically on a single sliver of silicon

Moore's law
the prediction (rather than a scientific 'law') that computer processing power would double, in terms of 'transistors per square inch', approximately every 18 months – see page 131

Neural network
when computers are configured to behave like a network of nerve cells

Operating system
the basic program which coordinates and organizes the computer's central processor, allowing it to carry out multiple tasks, run more than one user-facing program, and control peripheral devices like monitors and printers

Personal computer
a computing machine designed for use by a single individual, as contrasted with a mainframe used by multiple users within a large organisation

Polynomial
a mathematical expression typically taking the form $ax^n + bx^{n-1} + cx^{n-2} \dots$

Program
instructions given to a computing machine to carry out a specified task

Qubit
a 'quantum bit' – the equivalent in quantum computing to a bit (binary digit) in classical computing

Semiconductor
a metallic substance which conducts electricity, or acts as an insulator, depending on the conditions – typically used to enable electronic switching at a microscopic level

Social media
communications programs connecting communities into networks to share ideas, news and information

Stack overflow
running out of digits for storage of large numbers: so, if (in binary) 11001 is to be added to 10000 but the storage space can hold only five digits, the wrong answer 1001 will be recorded instead of the correct value 101001

Turing test
the classic test for determining whether a machine can think – see page 175

Index

Picture credits

We have made every effort to contact the copyright holders of the images used in this book. Any omissions will be rectified in future editions.

Advertising Archives: 93

AKG Images: 113 (bottom), 186 (top)

Alamy: 15, 140 (top), 191, 197, 199

American Computer & Robotics Museum, Bozeman, Montana: 88 (bottom)

AP Images: 184

Bridgeman Images: 13, 51–2

Diomedia: 174

Getty Images: 10–11, 48, 53 (top), 57, 60, 66, 73, 96, 97, 106 (top), 107 (bottom), 113 (top), 115, 118, 122, 123 (bottom), 130 (bottom), 132, 136, 144, 173, 180, 183 (top), 188, 189, 190 (top), 201 (top)

Giles Orr: 187

Iowa State University: 91, 92

John Romanishin: 193

King's College Cambridge: 58 (top), 59, 192

LEO Computers Society: 108 (bottom)

Library of Congress: 45, 82, 86–7,

Mary Evans Picture Library: 23 (top), 56

NASA: 104–5, 194–5

Rand Corporation/Paul Baran: 147

Science & Society: 41, 103, 143

Science Photo Library: 27, 32, 36, 39, 53 (bottom), 88 (top), 95, 131, 133 (bottom), 170–1

Shutterstock: 2, 6, 9 (x2), 12, 14 (x2), 16, 20, 21, 30–1, 35, 38, 44, 45 (top), 52, 58 (bottom), 64, 70, 72, 74, 81 (bottom), 83, 85, 101, 106 (bottom), 108 (top), 112, 117 (bottom), 120, 121, 124–5, 127 (x2), 128, 129 (top), 130 (top), 138, 139, 140 (bottom), 141, 143 (bottom), 145 (x2), 148, 150, 152, 155, 156–7, 158, 160 (x2; TWITTER, TWEET, RETWEET and the Twitter logo are trademarks of Twitter, Inc. or its affiliates.), 161 (bottom), 164 (x2), 165, 166, 172, 177 (x2), 178, 179, 181, 183 (bottom), 185 (top), 196 (x2), 200

Stanford News Service: 168

US Naval History and Heritage Command: 90

Wellcome Images: 26 (top), 28, 33

www.SiliconMaps.com: 169